SPANISH

AT HOME

Emma Warren

Spanish

Smith
Street
Books

at Home

Introd

If you're fortunate enough to have spent time in Spain, you will be familiar with its generous hospitality, rich cultural history and intensely regional gastronomy. It is a cuisine built on centuries of influence, invasion and imports: olive trees and grape vines introduced by the Phoenicians; citrus groves, fruit orchards, almonds, sugarcane, eggplants, rice and spices from the invading Moors, who established trade routes between the Middle East and western Mediterranean; and capsicums, tomatoes, potatoes and chocolate that arrived from the Americas, shortly after Christopher Columbus made landfall. Today, it is unimaginable to think of Spanish cuisine without these fundamental ingredients.

My love affair with Spanish food began while 'WWOOFING' (World Wide Opportunities on Organic Farms) through Spain. I learned to cook in the humble homes of many generous Spanish hosts in exchange for food and board. It opened my eyes to a cuisine I knew little about and propelled me into my career and life-long obsession with Spain, its people and, of course, its food. While travelling, it was the Basque Country that pulled me in the most. I was attracted to its rugged landscape and daily priorities that always centred around food. Living in a rural farmhouse, I'd spend the days building a vegetable garden for my host family, working quickly so I could come inside and help in the kitchen. This is where I discovered the resourcefulness and frugality of Spanish home

cooking, as well as its emphasis on minimal waste, from using steamed mussel liquor as stock for paellas, to deep-frying green leek tops to serve as a *pintxo* before lunch.

Further south, in Andalucía, I experienced *pueblo* cooking at outdoor village gatherings: paellas the size of small dams were prepared and cooked on top of enormous fires, stirred with boat oars and served up hot to the entire town. It was the perfect example of how human connection through food is a huge part of Spanish culture and a completely addictive way to live.

Spanish at Home might have you adding a little more olive oil than you're used to, or seeking out less familiar produce, but that's no bad thing. If you can, visit your nearest Spanish delicatessen and stock up on good-quality sherry vinegar, *bomba* rice for paella, varieties of pimentón and, of course, *jamón*. These basic ingredients will transform your dishes and understanding of Spanish home-cooking.

The recipes in this book are not the most famous Spain has to offer. Instead, they are a celebration of the homemade meals cooked in kitchens throughout the Iberian Peninsula and across the Spanish islands. It is what the locals eat, using the produce that surrounds them, paying homage to the land and the sea and the vegetable patch. It is food that is rich in history, diversity and cultural pride. It is flavourful and eclectic and, most of all, it is filled with the love of sharing food with others.

The Spanish kitchen pantry

Spain is famous for the quality of its produce, and here are some of the most important ingredients that you'll find in Spanish kitchens throughout the Iberian Peninsula and across the islands. Stock up on the below to give your Spanish home-cooking a bit of flamenco flair and a boost of authenticity.

Dried beans

Alubias secas (dried beans) are revered throughout Spain. From the heritage white *Ganxet* bean of Catalonia, to the larger *Asturias fabes de la granja* that forms the foundation of *fabada* – Spain's answer to cassoulet – dried white beans adorn every Spanish kitchen pantry. Take the time to soak dried beans in plenty of cold water overnight, and you'll be rewarded with a superior flavour and texture.

Garlic

Planted in autumn, harvested in spring and dried over summer, few Spanish meals are complete without the addition of *ajo* (garlic). The famous heirloom *roja* variety is sought after by restaurants across the world for its superior flavour. When selecting garlic, look for bulbs with firm necks for firmer, fresher cloves.

Jamón Iberico

Distinct from Italy's prosciutto, made from *jamón Serrano*, *jamón Iberico* comes from Spain's sacred Iberian black pig. Truly free range, Iberian pigs roam the Spanish countryside feeding primarily on grass that is supplemented with acorns, barley or corn in winter. The acorns are particularly important for adding the signature flavour and fat ratio that's so well-loved in *jamón Iberico*. The ageing time of the *jamón* ranges from 100 days to 36 months, which affects the texture and quality of the final product.

Ñora pepper

This small, bell-shaped dried pepper lends an earthy, sweet taste to sauces and tomato-based dishes. It is available from some specialty Spanish delicatessens, but if you can't find it, dried cascabel or ancho chillies can be substituted at a pinch. To prepare ñora peppers, soak them in warm water for 20 minutes to rehydrate, then scrape the flesh away from the skin and add to dishes, such as Catalan Romesco sauce.

Paella rice

The most popular variety of paella rice is *arroz bomba*. Due to a longer maturation and drying process, the small grains retain their shape and texture, while absorbing up to three times more liquid than other varieties of short-grain rice. Unlike arborio rice, *arroz bomba* is designed to hold onto its starch content under heat and hydration, resulting in an al dente paella that's neither creamy nor mushy.

Pimentón

Sweet, hot and smoked pimentóns are essential in Spanish cooking, where they are used for their vibrancy as much as their flavour. Pimentón is added to cured meats, such as chorizo and sobrassada, and sauces and one-pan dishes, including sofrito, paella and slow-cooked stews. It is irreplaceable in Spanish cuisine, so seek out the best-quality you can afford.

Sobrassada

This soft, spreadable, fermented pork sausage is more akin to a pate than a chorizo, and more versatile, too. With Sicilian roots, sobrassada is a centuries-old cured meat that is still eaten throughout the Balearic Islands where it is spread on toast, served with eggs, added to stews and pasta dishes and even eaten with honey. Look for it in specialty Spanish delicatessens.

Vinegars

Vinagre de Jerez (sherry vinegar) is uniquely Spanish. It has a smooth, dry and well-rounded acidic taste that complements many savoury dishes. It's well worth seeking out a good-quality brand to add depth of flavour to your meals. White and red wine vinegars are more neutral in flavour and generally used for pickling, marinating, making salad dressings and serving with quality tinned seafood.

snacks

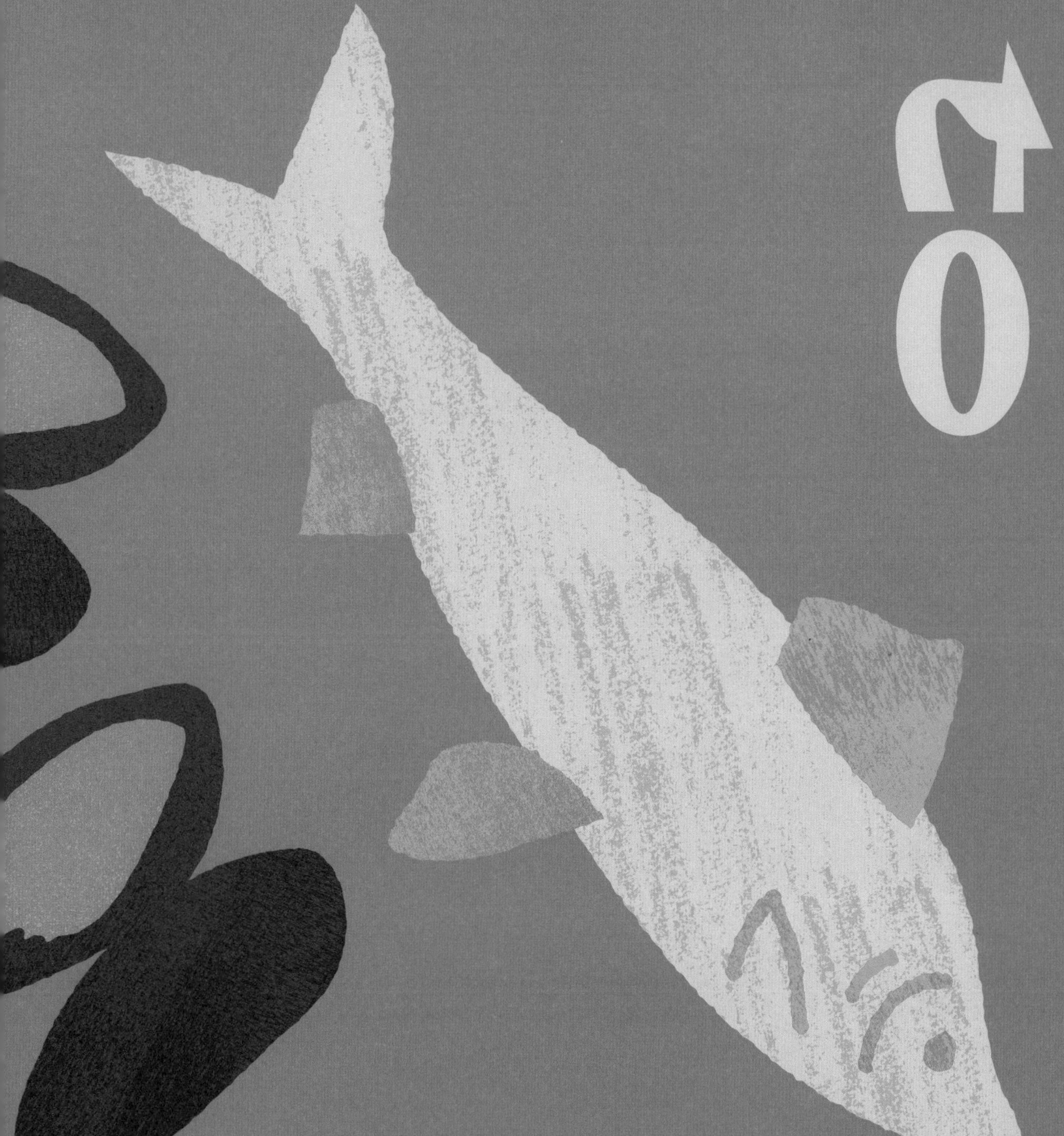

to

Share

 If you've ever been to Spain, you'll know that many of the country's most famous dishes are designed to share. From the northern-western tip of the country in the rugged province of Galicia down to the eclectic Canary Islands off the coast of Morocco and all the way across the mainland, coming together for a meal, or simply gathering at the local bar for a few drinks, is not complete without a selection of bite-sized snacks for everyone to enjoy.

Most of us are familiar with tapas, and their even tinier cousin pinchos, but the array of smaller dishes available extends beyond the distinctly Spanish culture of small plates displayed on wooden counters for you to help yourself and generally consume standing up.

In Spanish homes, it is traditional to 'open the appetite' with a few salty, crispy, flavourful bits and pieces to gain a time advantage that allows you to finish cooking the main attraction without any hunger-fuelled interruptions. Huddled around an informal plate of white anchovies, some fried nuts, juicy olives or a slice of *coca*, while catching up with friends and family around the kitchen table is a quintessential part of the Spanish home-cooked meal.

Handing out a few deep-fried morsels, such as artichoke chips, stuffed mussels, *patatas bravas* or some cod fritters – along with a basket of sliced bread that can double up as a napkin – is the perfect way to begin any Spanish feast, and really exemplifies the social aspects that so many of us love about the Spanish food scene.

So before you fire up the paella pan, gather your friends, pour some sangria and tuck into a selection of Spanish snacks straight from the streets. Oh, and don't forget the finger bowls!

Out of the more than 100 types of almonds grown in Spain, the Marcona, 'Queen of Almonds', is a native botanical variety characterised by its round, flat shape and soft texture. Inside its hard, non-porous exterior lies a high level of concentrated oils, making it a rich, intensely flavoured, sweet and juicy nut. Outside of Spain, Marcona often refers to the skinless, toasted, salted snack widely marketed throughout the rest of Europe and the US, even though the almonds used may not be their original varietal namesake.

This dish is traditionally served as an aperitif or snack, but the almonds can also be chopped and sprinkled over salads or braised meats, added to salted caramel toffees and stuffed dates or old-school devils on horsebacks.

Almendras Marconas

300 g (10½ oz) blanched
    almonds
1½ tablespoons extra virgin
    olive oil
1 sprig of rosemary
1 garlic clove, smashed
2 teaspoons butter
1 teaspoon salt flakes

Place the almonds in a large bowl, cover with lukewarm water and allow to stand for 1 hour. This will rehydrate any old, dry almonds and enable them to absorb more flavours in the pan.

Drain and spread the almonds in a single, even layer on a clean tea towel or paper towel and leave to air-dry for about 20 minutes. Alternatively, put the almonds in a very low 60°C (140°F) fan-forced oven for 6 minutes to dry out.

Heat the olive oil, rosemary and garlic in a large saucepan or frying pan over medium–high heat. Toss through the almonds and stir to toast evenly.

Once the almonds start to turn golden, add the butter, swirl the pan to coat and continue to cook for 2 minutes.

Remove the pan from the heat, stir through the salt flakes, then briefly drain the almond mixture on paper towel. Transfer to a serving bowl and serve immediately while the almonds are still warm.

Arbequina olives are some of the most juicy, buttery, peppery and oil-rich varieties of olive. Grown mainly in and around the volcanic mineral-rich area of Les Garrigues, Lleida, the olives originally take their name from the small village of Arbeca, where 1000-year-old trees are still in harvest. Due to their high fat content, Arbequina olives are ideal for oil production, but their small but meaty and nutty flesh makes for a great table olive, too. You will often find them served in their own oil, with a mix of wild herbs picked from the surrounding hills where the olive trees thrive.

Olivas Arbequinas

400 g (14 oz) brined Arbequina olives, wild olives or good-quality mixed olives

peel of ½ orange, pith removed

2 sprigs of thyme

2 fresh bay leaves

2 sprigs of marjoram or oregano

1 teaspoon aniseed or 1 star anise

1 teaspoon fennel seeds

2 garlic cloves, quartered

2 fennel fronds (optional)

80 ml (⅓ cup) extra virgin olive oil

crusty bread, to serve

Drain the olives from their brine and place in a large bowl. Cut the orange peel into strips and add to the bowl, along with the remaining ingredients, except the olive oil.

Warm the olive oil in a large saucepan or frying pan over low heat. Add the olive mixture and gently warm through, stirring constantly, for 8–10 minutes, until the flavours have infused.

Transfer to a serving bowl and serve the olives warm, with ripped crusty bread to mop up the flavour-filled oil.

Boqueróns (anchovies) are loved throughout Spain. The small, oily fish are caught along the Spanish Mediterranean coastline and then preserved in either salt (to make the salted anchovies you buy in jars), or vinegar to make boquerones. This popular Spanish tapa is often eaten as the ultimate aperitif during late Sunday morning vermouth sessions with mates, debriefing about the *discoteca* the night before. A lot of bars serve boquerones with a small plate of homemade *patata* crisps doused in spicy sauce and some stuffed olives on the house, to get you back on track before everyone disperses to their parents' house for Sunday family lunch.

Boquerones

150–200 g (5½–7 oz) white anchovies in vinegar

2½ tablespoons extra virgin olive oil

1 teaspoon sweet pimentón

1 dried ñora pepper, rehydrated in hot water, seeds removed and sliced into strips (see page 8)

160 g (5½ oz) bag good-quality salted potato chips (crisps)

Tabasco or Mexican hot sauce, for drizzling

green olives, stuffed with pimientos, to serve

Pat the anchovies dry with paper towel. Transfer to a glass or ceramic dish and drizzle with the oil. Sprinkle over the pimentón and dried pepper strips.

Tip the potato chips into a bowl and drizzle with the hot sauce.

Serve the anchovies and chips with the stuffed olives and a glass of red vermouth with loads of ice and a wedge of orange.

This recipe is a really interesting way to make stuffed mussels, using the mussel shell as a ready-made spoon. You can add scallops, prawns (shrimp) or any seafood or crustacean to the mix here.

These little stars are served a lot at special family gatherings, and in San Sebastian where the local Basque taverns make them as a clever way to use up leftover cooked mussels.

Tigres

2 eggs, beaten

2 tablespoons full-cream (whole) milk

150 g (1 cup) plain (all-purpose) flour

sourdough or panko breadcrumbs, to crumb

2 tablespoons chopped tarragon or parsley

salt flakes and freshly cracked black pepper

1 litre (4 cups) rice bran, grapeseed or vegetable oil

lemon wedges, to serve

Mussels

250 ml (1 cup) white wine

1 fresh bay leaf

2 sprigs of thyme, leaves picked and chopped

1 teaspoon peppercorns

1 kg (2 lb 3 oz) mussels, scrubbed and debearded

pinch of salt flakes

Béchamel

500 ml (2 cups) full-cream (whole) milk

1 fresh bay leaf

3 tablespoons plain (all-purpose) flour

60 ml (¼ cup) extra virgin olive oil

For the mussels, heat a large, deep frying pan or wok with a lid over high heat. Add the white wine, bay leaf, thyme and peppercorns and bring to a simmer. Add the mussels and salt, then cover and steam for 3–4 minutes, until the mussels open. Discard any mussels that remain closed.

Using a slotted spoon, remove the mussels from the pan and transfer to a bowl. Reserve the cooking liquid for the béchamel. Remove the mussels from their shells and reserve the 12 best, unbroken, equal-sized shells for the filling. Roughly chop the mussel meat and set aside.

To make the béchamel, heat the milk, bay leaf and 2½ tablespoons of the reserved mussel cooking liquid until it starts to steam – do not let the mixture boil. Remove the bay leaf and discard. In another small saucepan, heat the flour and oil over low heat and stir to make a roux. Once the roux starts to sizzle and take on a sandy texture, add the warmed milk mixture and whisk rapidly to avoid lumps. Keep whisking for 5–7 minutes, until the béchamel becomes smooth and thick. Fold through the chopped mussels and spoon the mixture into the reserved shells. Allow to cool before placing in the fridge for at least 1 hour to set.

Set up three small bowls: place the beaten egg and milk in one bowl; the flour in another bowl; and the breadcrumbs and herbs in the third bowl. Season the egg with salt and pepper.

Once set, pass the mussels and their shells through the flour, then the egg wash and finally the breadcrumbs.

Heat the oil in a deep-fryer or large saucepan to 185–190°C (365–375°F). Drop a breadcrumb into the hot oil; if it sizzles straight away, the oil is ready.

Working in batches, lower the stuffed mussels into the oil and fry for 4–6 minutes, until golden brown. Drain on paper towel and serve immediately with plenty of lemon wedges for squeezing over.

This is Catalonia's answer to pizza, except it's rectangular and has no cheese! All generations adore this slice of convenience, which is especially enjoyed on public holidays during festivals such as Semana Santa, La Mercè, Sant Joan, La Diada and Navidad. On these occasions, a little sugar is often sprinkled over the top of more traditional ingredients, such as salty anchovies or sardines and smoky vegetables.

Similar to the French pissaladière, this popular dish is sold in local bakeries all year round and often with other, more modern toppings, such as ham and cheese, or spinach, raisins and pine nuts. Eaten hot, at room temperature or cold, it's a great picnic dish for the beach, park or a trip to the mountains.

Coca de verduras

180 ml (6 fl oz) lukewarm water

2 teaspoons active dried yeast

2 tablespoons extra virgin olive oil

½ teaspoon caster (superfine) sugar

350 g (2⅓ cups) plain (all-purpose) flour, plus extra for dusting

pinch of salt flakes

Toppings

olive oil, for brushing and drizzling

1 x quantity Escalivada (see page 217)

8 salted anchovy fillets

1 tablespoon baby capers

10 pitted black olives

1 teaspoon caster (superfine) sugar

Preheat the oven to 220°C (430°F) fan-forced. Line a baking tray with baking paper.

Combine the water, yeast, oil and sugar in a small jug and allow to stand for 5 minutes at room temperature.

Place the flour and salt in a large bowl. Once the yeast mixture starts to froth, slowly mix it into the flour until a rough dough forms. Transfer the dough to a well-floured work surface and knead for 5 minutes or until you have a smooth, firm dough. Place the dough on the prepared tray, cover with a clean and ever-so slightly damp tea towel and leave to rest at room temperature for 15–20 minutes, until it has risen by one-third.

Divide the dough into two or four balls, depending on your preference. Working with one piece of dough at a time and keeping the remaining dough covered with the tea towel, use a rolling pin to roll the dough into a rough rectangle shape, about 6 mm (¼ in) thick. Transfer to the baking tray (you may need two trays) and repeat with the remaining dough.

Brush the dough lightly with olive oil, then arrange the escalivada in alternating strips across the top in an even layer. Drape over the anchovies, followed by the capers and black olives. Sprinkle with the sugar and bake for 12–15 minutes, depending on the size of your pizzas.

To serve, drizzle the pizzas with a little extra olive oil, cut into random pieces and eat straight off the tray.

Spain has a long history of pickling and preserving good-quality fish and meat. Now famous, these products are often expensive and prized throughout the country and further afield. The sweet and sour ingredients in this recipe lend themselves to the stronger flavours of game birds, such as pheasant, partridge, pigeon and quail, and oily fish, such as sardines, tuna, bonito, salmon and trout – even eel works well. Here, the mackerel gently absorbs the acid while it cools and preserves, which really mellows out the intense flavour.

Escabeche de caballa

4 x 200 g (7 oz) small mackerel, filleted (you can also use sardines or an 800 g/ 1 lb 12 oz side of Spanish mackerel, cut into 4 fillets)

145 ml (5 fl oz) extra virgin olive oil

salt flakes

12 Dutch carrots, peeled and tops trimmed, thicker carrots sliced in half lengthways

½ fennel bulb, sliced

2 shallots, thickly sliced

2 garlic cloves, halved, germ removed

2 fresh bay leaves

2 sprigs of thyme

10 pink peppercorns

10 white peppercorns

½ teaspoon coriander seeds

½ teaspoon sweet pimentón

125 ml (½ cup) sherry or red wine vinegar

½ teaspoon caster (superfine) sugar

crusty baguette or rye bread, to serve

horseradish cream, to serve (optional)

Heat a non-stick frying pan over high heat. Drizzle the mackerel with 1 tablespoon of the oil, sprinkle with a little salt, then add to the pan and sear for 1 minute on each side.

Heat 60 ml (¼ cup) of the oil in a saucepan over medium heat and add the carrots, fennel, shallot, garlic, bay leaves, thyme, peppercorns and coriander seeds. Gently cook for 5–6 minutes, until the vegetables just start to soften. Remove from the heat and stir through the pimentón, vinegar, ½ teaspoon of salt and the sugar.

Transfer the mackerel to a heatproof dish and pour over the vegetables and warm escabeche marinade to cover the fish. Stand at room temperature for a minimum of 2 hours for the vinegar flavours to penetrate the fish before serving or, even better, leave to cool for 20–30 minutes, then refrigerate overnight and serve the following day.

Serve at room temperature with a crusty baguette or on rye bread as an aperitivo. A little dollop of horseradish cream on top is also special.

Silverbeet doughnuts

These bite-sized joys are traditionally served as a dessert, but adding a little garlic and cumin turns them into a really quirky starter or appetiser. Add a squeeze of lemon at the end, along with a sprinkling of salt and a drizzle of honey, and your guests will start to wonder what stage of the meal they're at! And if you're still hungry after an evening of feasting, you can have one for dessert as well. If there's any left ...

Buñuelos de acelgas

300 g (10½ oz) silverbeet (Swiss chard), stalks removed

iced water

150 g (1 cup) plain (all-purpose) flour

2 eggs

150 ml (5 fl oz) full-cream (whole) milk

1 tablespoon caster (superfine) sugar

½ teaspoon baking powder

2 garlic cloves, crushed

large handful of parsley, leaves finely chopped

½ teaspoon ground cumin

salt flakes and freshly cracked black pepper

1 litre (4 cups) rice bran, grapeseed or vegetable oil

2 tablespoons honey

juice of ½ lemon

your favourite hard cheese, to serve

green olives, to serve

Slice the silverbeet leaves as thinly as possible. Rinse well in iced water, then drain and set aside on a clean tea towel to dry.

Combine the flour, eggs, milk, sugar and baking powder in a bowl to make a batter. Fold through the garlic, parsley, cumin, a pinch of salt and pepper and the silverbeet leaves, then set aside for 10 minutes.

Heat the vegetable oil in a large heavy-based saucepan to 180°C (350°F) on a kitchen thermometer. Working in batches, spoon tablespoons of the batter into the oil and fry for 2–3 minutes each side until golden (they are so light, they usually turn themselves over). Using a slotted spoon, transfer the doughnuts to a tray lined with paper towel.

Place the doughnuts on a large serving plate, sprinkle with extra salt and drizzle over the honey and lemon. Serve with a big slab of your favourite hard cheese and a few olives, and get ready to lick your fingers.

Originally from Andalucia, these addictive morsels get washed down all summer long in bars, *chiringuitos* (beach bars) and poolside with a beer or two between dips. I love scooping them up with a really hot English mustard alioli, which is also popular with German and British tourists who, along with beer, love a spicy condiment!

Alcachofas rebozadas

8–10 small artichokes, hard outer leaves removed

fine sea salt

1 lemon, halved

150 g (1 cup) plain (all-purpose) flour

90 g (½ cup) potato flour or rice flour

½ teaspoon baking powder

250 ml (1 cup) ice-cold lager

1 free-range egg

1 litre (4 cups) rice bran, grapeseed or vegetable oil

salt flakes

unpitted black olives, to serve

Mustard alioli

2 garlic cloves

80 g (⅓ cup) good-quality egg mayonnaise

2 teaspoons hot English mustard

Trim the artichoke stalks, leaving 2 cm (¾ in) attached. Peel the outer layer of the stalks with a vegetable peeler.

Bring a large saucepan of water to the boil and season well with salt. Add the trimmed artichokes and one lemon half squeezed in, and blanch for 6–8 minutes, until the artichokes are just under-cooked and still a little firm. Remove from the pan and pat dry with a clean tea towel, squeezing out as much moisture as possible. Discard the lemon half.

Cut the artichokes in half and remove the fibrous choke, then cut into 5 mm (¼ in) thick slices.

Combine half the plain flour, the potato or rice flour, baking powder and ½ teaspoon of fine sea salt in a large bowl. Slowly pour in the beer, whisking constantly to avoid any lumps, then beat in the egg until the batter has a thick-cream consistency.

Heat the vegetable oil in a deep frying pan to 180°C (350°F) on a kitchen thermometer.

Meanwhile, make the mustard alioli. In a small bowl, finely grate the garlic into the mayonnaise and stir through the mustard. Set aside.

Dust the artichoke slices with the remaining plain flour, then dip in the batter to coat. Working in batches, fry the artichoke for 2–3 minutes, until golden, then transfer to a tray lined with paper towel and sprinkle with salt flakes before the excess oil drips off.

Serve the artichoke chips with the mustard alioli and a few olives on the side.

<u>Salted cod fritters</u>

These fritters are usually eaten as a special Sunday-morning tapa before the main meal. *Buñuelo* is a colloquial term for something badly done or when something has not turned out as expected. A lot of great dishes in history have evolved from mistakes or errors, and these small imperfect balls of perfection are a favourite in many Spanish families.

There are a few different techniques to making these balls of bacalao (salt cod). The most effective way I've found is to make them similar to a churros pastry, with eggs, or a choux pastry mix, for a fluffier, pillow-like result. You can make the mixture the day before, if you like.

Buñuelos de bacalao

300 g (10½ oz) prepared bacalao (salt cod) fillets (see method on page 125)

200 g (7 oz) desiree or other floury potato, peeled and chopped

2 sprigs of thyme

2 tablespoons extra virgin olive oil

80 g (2¾ oz) plain (all-purpose) flour

2 eggs

1 garlic clove, minced

2 tablespoons chopped parsley leaves

salt flakes and ground white pepper

1 litre (4 cups) rice bran, grapeseed or vegetable oil

lemon wedges, to serve

Alioli (see page 256), to serve (optional)

Place the bacalao in a saucepan and cover with plenty of cold water. Bring to a simmer over medium heat and poach for 3 minutes, then remove from the heat and allow to sit for 10 minutes.

Remove the bacalao using a slotted spoon and set aside in a large bowl. Add the potato and thyme to the poaching liquid, return the pan to medium heat and bring to the boil. Reduce the heat to a simmer and cook the potato until soft. Strain the potato and add to the bacalao, reserving the cooking liquid for the batter. Discard the thyme sprigs.

Bring 150 ml (5 fl oz) of the reserved cooking liquid, 150 ml (5 fl oz) of water and the olive oil to the boil in a saucepan. Remove from the heat and gently rain in the flour, whisking to avoid any lumps, until thickened and smooth. Allow to cool slightly before whisking in the eggs, one at a time, until incorporated.

Mash the potato and bacalao as much as you can – it's fine to have a few lumps of fish – and stir through the garlic and parsley.

Place the pan with the batter over low heat and, using a wooden spoon or spatula, fold through the bacalao and potato mixture. Cook gently for 10 minutes or until a thick batter forms and starts to come away from the base and side of the pan. Taste the mixture and adjust the seasoning with salt flakes and a little white pepper. Allow the batter to cool a little, then transfer to a large bowl and refrigerate until completely cold (this makes the batter easier to handle and prevents the balls sticking together when frying).

Heat the oil in a saucepan to 185–190°C (365–375°F) on a kitchen thermometer.

Using two tablespoons, form the batter into 15–20 rough balls. Working in batches, carefully lower 5–6 balls into the hot oil and cook for 2–3 minutes each side, until golden. Drain on paper towel. Serve with lemon wedges and a good dollop of alioli, if you like.

Literally meaning 'brave potatoes', patatas bravas are doused in a very garlicky alioli followed by an extremely spicy red sauce. They are generally only eaten as tapa, often shared with friends or family at a street-side terrace bar. The last potato is called *la patata de verguenza* (the shameful potato). The mere mention of this one last lonely *brava* has the 'bravest' of the group jumping to declare their lack of shame and hastily eating what's left in the bowl.

Some bars serve fat patatas bravas, whereas others prefer small and crispy potatoes, but I think a bit of both is always good; those burnt little crispy bits, which contrast the warm starchy mouthfuls of potato soaked in sauce, are delicious.

Patatas bravas

60 ml (¼ cup) extra virgin olive oil

½ onion, finely diced or grated

2 small red chillies, chopped

pinch of salt flakes

2 teaspoons smoked pimentón

1 teaspoon spicy pimentón

2 teaspoons cayenne pepper

3 tablespoons plain (all-purpose) flour

1 tablespoon sherry vinegar

650 ml (22 fl oz) chicken stock

5 medium sebago, king edward or russet potatoes, peeled and cut into 3–4 cm (1¼–1½ in) uneven chunks

1 litre (4 cups) rice bran, grapeseed or vegetable oil

1 x quantity Alioli (see page 256)

Heat the olive oil in a frying pan over medium heat, add the onion, chilli and salt, then reduce the heat to low and slowly sweat the onion for 5–7 minutes, until translucent. Add both pimentóns and the cayenne and stir well. Add the flour and cook, stirring, for 1 minute or until you have a roux consistency. Add the sherry vinegar, then gradually pour in the stock, whisking constantly to avoid any lumps. Once all the stock has been added, simmer gently for about 10 minutes, until thickened. Remove the pan from the heat and blend the sauce with a hand-held blender until smooth and lump-free. Pass the sauce through a fine sieve for a perfect silky finish. Set aside to cool, then transfer the sauce to a squeeze bottle or clean tomato ketchup bottle.

Pat dry the potato with a clean tea towel and place in a deep frying pan with the oil. Make sure both the potato and oil are at room temperature.

Bring the oil to a rolling simmer over medium–high heat, stirring occasionally to prevent the starchy potatoes sticking. Cook for 12–15 minutes, until the potato begins to turn golden. Using a slotted spoon, scoop out a potato chunk and make sure that it's cooked all the way through. Strain off the oil, then drain the potato on paper towel. Transfer the potato to a serving bowl, sprinkle with salt flakes and douse in the red sauce and alioli. Dig in with small forks or toothpicks.

 Throughout Spain, the days are longer than elsewhere in Europe. Shops, bars and restaurants lift their shutters mid-morning and stay open until late at night, breaking in the middle of the day for the ubiquitous *siesta* to escape the heat of the afternoon sun. As a result of this more relaxed approach, the Spanish don't usually eat breakfast and wait until 'brunch time' to enjoy a more substantial meal. In fact, it could be said that the Spanish have been brunching far longer than other cultures.

Those that do hit the road early may only have enough time or energy to manage a strong espresso (perhaps with some rum in it) and a pastry. Otherwise, a traditional mid-morning meal might involve a visit to the local bakery for bread to make the famous *pan con tomate* – an incredibly simple dish of toasted bread rubbed with raw garlic and smeared with over-ripe tomatoes, good-quality olive oil and salt.

That said, the more modern concept of a Western weekend brunch is starting to take hold, and the Spanish *almuerzo*, meaning 'morning tea' does serve up some of the more typical brunch offerings you see outside of the country, with plenty of larger savoury options that will see you through to late lunch.

The next time you have a sleep-in or wake up with a slight hangover from the night before, treat yourself to a relaxed morning and try one of the Iberian brunch dishes in this chapter to help kick-start your day. Consider the Cuban rice – a unique meal, complete with rice, egg, tomato sauce and banana (don't discount it until you've tried it!) to help get you back on your feet, or opt for something more traditional, such as baked eggs, a classic ham and cheese toastie that's loved throughout Barcelona or some deeply nourishing (and filling) baked beans, Spanish style.

Pan con tomate is a major part of the Spanish identity and relies completely on the quality of all five ingredients. Garlic is rubbed onto the surface of coarse, crusty bread, followed by juicy ripe tomatoes, a good drizzle of new-season cold-pressed olive oil and finally a gush of sea salt. The dish is a longstanding favourite for most Spaniards (who have been 'brunching' far longer than most cultures) although it's also eaten at lunch and dinner. There are even tomatoes grown specifically to ripen in winter so locals can enjoy their beloved pan con tomate all year round.

Pan con tomate

4 slices rustic sourdough
    white bread

1 garlic clove, peeled

2 very ripe tomatoes, halved

1 tablespoon extra virgin
    olive oil

1 teaspoon salt flakes

Toast, grill or barbecue the bread slowly to dry it out and harden it slightly. Gently rub the garlic clove over each slice – the abrasiveness of the toasted bread will cut the garlic across its surface.

Firmly squash the tomato onto the bread, cut side down, and squeeze as you rub to release the juice and flesh.

Drizzle with olive oil, sprinkle evenly with salt and *bon profiti!*

These simple and contrasting flavours – sweet, floral honey and intensely strong-flavoured sobrassada – are an exquisite combination unique to Spain. In addition to spreading it on toast for a classic Iberian-style brunch, you can also use this partnership to baste fish, chicken or stuffed mushrooms, or smear atop a canapé with a fried quail's egg on top.

Pan tostada con sobrassada y miel

½ loaf light rye bread

4 thick slices sobrassada
    (see page 8)

1 tablespoon floral honey

olive oil, for drizzling

caper berries, to serve

Preheat a grill (broiler) to high.

Cut the bread into four thick slices and grill on both sides until lightly toasted. Top each piece with a slice of sobrassada and gently spread to the edges. Return the toast to the grill and cook until the sobrassada has melted.

Transfer to plates and drizzle with the honey and oil. Serve with caper berries on the side.

This dish is the go-to hangover brunch when it's too much to bear cooking the ritual Sunday paella. The *tomate frito* is a supermarket product found in every Spanish household pantry, and many households cook exclusively with this fried tomato sauce, but I've included a quick homemade version here. Don't be put off by the unusual mix of ingredients in this dish, it really is the perfect combination of salty and sweet to cure even the most brutal of hangovers.

Arroz Cubano

2 tablespoons extra virgin olive oil

2 garlic cloves, smashed

1 fresh bay leaf

440 g (2 cups) short-grain rice, such as bomba or calasparra, rinsed and drained

pinch of sea salt

4 eggs

2 bananas, halved lengthways

1 teaspoon dried oregano

salt flakes and freshly cracked black pepper

Tomate frito

80 ml (⅓ cup) extra virgin olive oil

1½ tablespoons tomato paste (concentrated purée)

2 x 400 g (14 oz) tins chopped tomatoes

¼ teaspoon salt flakes

¼ teaspoon sugar

To make the tomate frito, heat the olive oil in a saucepan over medium heat, add the tomato paste and stir through the oil for 4–6 minutes, until beginning to colour. Add the chopped tomatoes, salt and sugar and stir through until starting to bubble. Reduce the heat to low and gently simmer for 20 minutes. Remove from the heat and blitz using a hand-held blender. Set aside in the saucepan and keep warm.

Heat 2 teaspoons of the olive oil in a saucepan over medium–high heat, add the garlic and bay leaf and stir through until starting to sizzle. Stir the rice into the pan, add the salt and pour in 950 ml (32 fl oz) of water. Cover and bring to the boil, then reduce the heat immediately to medium–low and gently simmer for 8–10 minutes, until nearly all the water has been absorbed. Turn off the heat and let the rice stand for 5 minutes.

Meanwhile, heat the remaining oil in a frying pan over medium heat and fry the eggs and banana.

Spoon the rice into shallow bowls and top with a big ladle of tomate frito. Add the banana and egg and sprinkle with dried oregano, salt flakes and freshly cracked black pepper.

Introduced by the dance club Sala Bikini in the 1950s, located in Barcelona's Les Corts district (which is also home to the Camp Nou football stadium), 'el bikini' is a popular late-night/early-morning post-nightclub snack famous throughout Catalonia. This simple ham and cheese toastie is sold in every bar, especially around universities and schools, where it's also the ultimate student morning tea, lunch or afternoon snack.

You can elevate its status by replacing the ham off the bone with *jamón ibérico* and using manchego or even shaved truffle, but there's something about keeping it simple, just the way I remember inhaling it: a crispy, thin, sweet, white-breaded, salty toastie in three or four bites in the early morning in Bar Estudiantil on Plaça de la Universitat, after a night of dancing at local club La Paloma to sign off the night as complete.

El bikini

2 tablespoons butter, softened

4 slices high-top sandwich bread, any quality or grain you like

4 thin slices sweet ham off the bone, such as champagne or Grandmother's ham

4 thin slices havarti (or similar semi-soft, mild white cow's cheese, such as asiago or muenster)

Heat a sandwich press to medium or a large frying pan over medium heat.

Spread the butter on both sides of the bread. Top two slices with the ham and cheese, then enclose with the remaining slices of bread.

Transfer the sandwiches to the sandwich press or frying pan and toast, flipping occasionally if using the frying pan, for 4–5 minutes, until the toasties are golden and crisp and the cheese has melted. (Keep the temperature at a medium heat – if it's too low you'll lose all of your cheese, and if it's too high you'll burn the bread.)

Cut the toasties in half diagonally and serve with a couple of paper napkins.

The modernist town of Sóller in the northwest of Mallorca is described as 'an island within an island'. Once isolated by the Tramuntana mountains, Sóller sits in the heart of the Golden Valley, a large citrus-growing area with a historical trade connection to France via the nearby Port de Sóller.

This French-inspired, yet entirely unique, baked-egg dish is famous throughout Sóller and takes pride of place on every cafe and bar menu, as well as being a favourite in the family home. For a lighter, vegetarian option, omit the sobrassada and add a teaspoon of sweet pimentón. It still delivers a wonderful flavour that's completely different from the usual tomato and bean base.

Huevos de Sóller

1 tablespoon extra virgin olive oil

1 garlic clove, smashed

1 carrot, finely diced

1 celery stalk, finely diced

1 leek, white part only, finely chopped

80 ml (⅓ cup) dry white wine or dry sherry

300 ml (10 fl oz) chicken or vegetable stock

500 g (1 lb 2 oz) frozen peas

salt flakes and ground white pepper

4 thick slices sobrassada (see page 8)

8 eggs

crusty bread, to serve

Preheat the oven to 200°C (400°F) fan-forced.

Heat the olive oil and garlic in a frying pan over medium heat. Add the carrot, celery and leek and cook for 10 minutes or until the vegetables are just beginning to colour and soften. Splash the wine into the pan and simmer until the liquid evaporates, then pour in the stock and bring to the boil. Reduce the heat and simmer for 5 minutes.

Stir all but 50 g (1¾ oz) of the peas into the pan and cook for 1 minute. Remove from the heat and season to taste with salt and white pepper. Transfer the mixture to a blender and blend to a smooth purée.

Pass the pea purée through a fine sieve into a bowl, then transfer the bowl to an ice bath, stirring to release the heat (this helps to maintain the green colour).

Place the sobrassada along one side of a large pie dish (or two smaller dishes) and spoon in enough purée to just cover the base of the rest of the dish. Crack the eggs on top of the pea purée and sprinkle over the remaining peas. Cover with a lid or foil and bake for 6–8 minutes for a soft yolk or 10 minutes if you prefer your eggs well done.

Meanwhile, reheat the remaining purée. Spoon the purée over the baked eggs, sprinkle with a little more pepper and serve with a big chunk of crusty bread on the side.

Gravy is a culinary hangover from the British. It arrived with the Royal Navy and stayed on the plates of locals, and is still served today with macaroni or fideos, and legumes and pulses such as lentils and chickpeas. This dish traditionally uses white beans or kidney beans (or a mixture of the two), but here I've used borlotti beans, which add a slightly nutty creaminess. It's worth making your own beef stock, too, with really well-roasted veal bones to enrich this original 'baked beans and gravy' experience.

Alubias en salsa 'gravy'

300 g (10½ oz) dried borlotti (cranberry) beans, soaked in cold water overnight, drained

1 sprig of rosemary

1 kg (2 lb 3 oz) beef marrowbones, oxtail or knuckle bones

20 g (¾ oz) butter

2 tablespoons extra virgin olive oil

1 field mushroom, roughly chopped

2 onions, roughly chopped

1 carrot, roughly chopped

1 garlic bulb, halved crossways

1 fresh bay leaf

2 tablespoons tomato paste (concentrated purée)

salt flakes and freshly cracked black pepper

2 litres (68 fl oz) Fondo oscuro de ternera (see page 263) or store-bought beef stock

2 thick English-style, good-quality pork sausages, sliced

1 sprig of marjoram or oregano

1½ tablespoons plain (all-purpose) flour

2 tomatoes, diced

4 poached eggs (optional)

Place the beans in a large saucepan with the rosemary. Cover with plenty of cold water and bring to the boil. Simmer over medium heat for 40–50 minutes, until the beans are tender. Drain. Remove and discard the rosemary sprig.

Meanwhile, place the beef marrowbones, butter and half the olive oil in a large stockpot over high heat. Stir the bones to coat in the butter and oil and cook for 10–15 minutes, until they have leached out their juices and turned grey with no blood remaining. Add the mushroom, half the onion, the carrot, garlic, bay leaf and tomato paste and season with salt and pepper. Cook for 10–12 minutes, until the ingredients have turned a dark golden brown. Pour in the stock, bring to the boil, then reduce the heat and gently simmer for 1 hour to let the flavours marry.

Strain the stock into a saucepan and keep warm.

Heat the remaining oil in a large heavy-based frying pan over medium–high heat. Add the sausage and marjoram or oregano and cook for 5 minutes or until the sausage is golden brown. Add the remaining onion and cook for 12–15 minutes, until soft and golden, then add the flour and stir for just under 1 minute to coat the onion. Slowly pour in the stock, stirring to combine, then add the beans. Bring to a simmer, stir through the tomato and cook for 2–3 minutes, until soft.

Serve the gravy beans in bowls, with a poached egg on top, if you like.

This Mallorcan dish is very popular among the locals. Like the trampó salad on page 137, everything is cut up into equal-sized pieces, small enough so you can fit several ingredients in your mouth at once. The fennel really is a cleanser to the lamb's liver, so even if you think you're not a fan of offal, you might be pleasantly surprised! You could also add more chilli to balance the liver, as this is one of the few spicy dishes on the island, although ease off if you're making it for a local. If you really do object to that strong liver taste, just substitute the offal with more diced lamb and it will still be amazing.

Think of this dish as a Spanish stir-fry. It's best to use a wide-based saucepan, frying pan, wok or even a paella pan to give everything the space it needs to fry instead of sweating too much. Also, 'jump' the pan as you go to keep the ingredients moving.

Frito

80 ml (⅓ cup) light-flavoured olive oil

80 ml (⅓ cup) extra virgin olive oil

4 potatoes, peeled and cut into 1 cm (½ in) dice

1 onion, diced

4 garlic cloves, unpeeled, smashed

salt flakes

2 teaspoons dry white wine

½ green capsicum (bell pepper), cut into 1 cm (½ in) dice

½ red capsicum (bell pepper), cut into 1 cm (½ in) dice

1 small fennel bulb, cut into 1 cm (½ in) dice, fronds reserved

1 small eggplant (aubergine), peeled in stripes lengthways, cut into 1 cm (½ in) dice

1 salad onion, diced

1 fresh bay leaf

2 sprigs of marjoram or oregano

1–2 long red chillies, thickly sliced

200 g (7 oz) boneless lamb shoulder or leg, cut into 1 cm (½ in) dice

200 g (7 oz) lamb's or calf's liver, finely diced

freshly cracked black pepper

Combine the oils in a jug and heat half the mixture in a large heavy-based saucepan over medium–high heat. Add the potato, onion, garlic and a pinch of salt and fry for 10–12 minutes, until the potato begins to soften and take on a golden colour.

Add the wine, capsicums, fennel, eggplant, salad onion, herbs and half the chilli, then increase the heat just a touch and cook for 12–15 minutes, stirring every few minutes to fry everything evenly without burning.

Meanwhile, in a separate frying pan, heat the remaining oil over high heat. Add the lamb and cook for 5 minutes, then add the liver with a pinch of salt and cook, stirring constantly, for 2 minutes, making sure not to overcook the liver. Strain off the oil in the pan and transfer the meat to the pan with the vegetables. Reduce the heat to medium and stir to bring everything together. Finish with the reserved fennel fronds and a little salt and pepper. Serve with the rest of the chilli scattered over the top, or more if you're keen.

This brioche cake can be found on hotel breakfast buffet menus and in bakeries throughout Mallorca. It's traditionally made using potatoes, which grow better on the island than grains, and they add a moist density to this unique cake. Use any seasonal fruit you like – apricots are traditional, but I sometimes mix it up a little with cherries, peaches and even pears.

Coca de patata con albaricoque

300 g (10½ oz) large potatoes

10 g (⅓ oz) active dried yeast

60 ml (¼ cup) full-cream (whole) milk, warmed

170 g (¾ cup) caster (superfine) sugar

3 free-range eggs

120 g (4½ oz) lard or unsalted butter, softened, plus extra for greasing

2 tablespoons olive oil, plus extra for greasing

1 teaspoon salt flakes

400 g (2⅔ cups) baker's flour

8–10 apricots, halved, stones removed

2 tablespoons granulated sugar

icing (confectioners') sugar, for dusting

Place the potatoes in a large saucepan and cover with cold water. Bring to the boil over high heat and cook for 30–35 minutes, until soft but not falling apart. Drain and set aside until cool enough to handle, then peel the skins and push the potato through a ricer or mouli into a large bowl while still warm.

Combine the yeast, warm milk and a teaspoon of the caster sugar in a small jug and set aside to activate.

Whisk the eggs in a large bowl, then whisk in the remaining caster sugar until pale and creamy. Add the lard or butter, olive oil, warm potato, salt and yeast mixture and mix well to combine. Rain in the flour a little at a time, incorporating it to form a sticky dough. Lightly grease your hands with oil and bring the dough together, kneading in the bowl to form a smooth, elastic ball. Cover with plastic wrap and set aside in a warm place for 1 hour or until risen by one-third.

Preheat the oven to 170°C (340°F) fan-forced. Line a 27 cm (10¾ in) cake tin (or a rectangular 32 x 22 cm/12¾ x 8¾ in tin) with baking paper and grease with a smidge of butter.

Transfer the dough to the tin and smooth the surface. Gently push the apricot halves, cut side down, into the dough, then set aside for a further 30–45 minutes, until risen by another one-third.

Sprinkle the granulated sugar over the top and bake for 30–35 minutes, until golden.

Remove from the oven and allow to cool before dusting the top with icing sugar. Slice and serve.

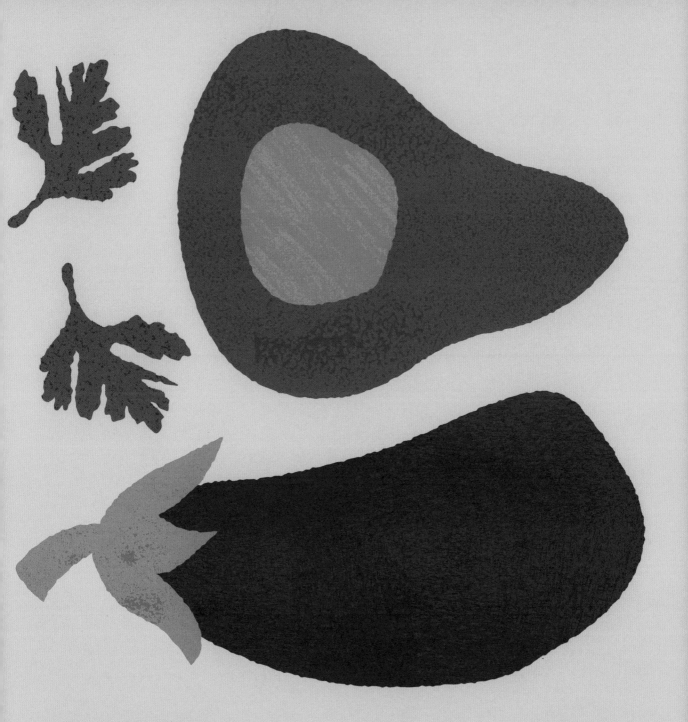

Fiesta

Summer is mid-year vacation time in Spain, and for the month of August most of the country's inland residents close up their houses and take to the beach for a long holiday. It is also the season of abundant produce, and the Spanish make the most of the glut by beginning and ending every meal with fresh vegetables and fruit, usually from a friend's or relative's garden.

For me, many summers were spent cooking in kitchens on the islands, catering for European and British tourists using market ingredients bought fresh that morning: hauls of gleaming fish straight from the local fishermen; bundles of summer vegetables, including multi-coloured ribbed tomatoes, heavy zucchini (courgettes) and eggplants (aubergines) for roasting or grilling; huge bunches of bitter greens waiting to be wilted and spritzed with lemon; and boxes of the sweetest, ripest fruit I have ever tasted.

Beating the heat usually involves eating less food more often, with lots of smaller tapas-style plates, cold soups and salads eaten throughout the day. Panzanella is one such popular dish, as is the lesser known, but extremely refreshing, cold melon soup. Vegetable and fish dishes abound, such as the layered fish and vegetable claypot bake *Cazuela de pescado al horno*. Of course, no Spanish summer feast would be complete without paella, and you'll find two in this chapter: a seafood paella broth and a more hearty paella made with fideos – Spain's answer to spaghetti – which guarantees you'll have leftovers the next day. Finally, the prawn cocktail may seem like a retro choice, but it is still popular in parts of Spain and I've included a decadant revival of the classic starter. Serve a few of these dishes together over a lazy al fresco lunch for a memorable summer feast with friends and family.

For dessert, fruit is typically served in summer, to aid digestion and allow the body to cope with that sensational afternoon heat.

In the late 1950s and early 60s, Spain's islands and mainland coastlines were a stomping ground for European and British celebrity elites and luxury travellers craving unforgettable sunsets and world-class beaches. From Marbella to Torremolinos on the Costa del Sol, many an eccentric writer, flamboyant musician and emerging artist could be spotted soaking up the southern sun, sipping on rum or strolling down the colourful esplanades. I can just imagine the upper echelons of society – a slim cigarette in one hand and a glass of shandy in the other – being served this popular (and now kitsch) dish, with its famous *salsa rosa*, poolside.

Cóctel de gambas

16 large cooked prawns (shrimp), peeled and deveined, tails left intact on 4 prawns

100 g (3½ oz) finely shredded iceberg lettuce

200 g (7 oz) honeydew melon or rockmelon (canteloupe), balled or cubed

¼ avocado, sliced lengthways

½ orange, thinly sliced

4 small sprigs of tarragon

Salsa rosa

80 g (⅓ cup) Mayonesa (see page 257)

2 tablespoons tomato ketchup

juice of ½ orange

2 teaspoons whisky or brandy

pinch of salt flakes and ground white pepper

¼ bunch of chives, finely snipped

Combine the salsa rosa ingredients in a small bowl.

Set aside the four prawns with their tails intact and roughly chop the remaining prawns into 1 cm (½ in) chunks. Fold the chopped prawn through the salsa rosa.

Arrange the shredded lettuce in the base of four cocktail, martini or dessert glasses and top with half the chopped prawn mixture. Divide the melon among the glasses and spoon the remaining prawn mixture on top. Gently place the avocado and orange slices upright in each glass. Finish with a prawn perched on top and sprinkle over the tarragon.

The Mediterranean culinary tradition of combining fresh fruit with cured meats lives on in this cold and refreshing soup from Catalonia that's perfect at the end of a hot day. You can make this recipe using rockmelon (cantaloupe), watermelon – even kiwi fruit works well – but I've opted for honeydew melon here. Be liberal when peeling the melon to make sure you remove all the bitter pith.

Sopa fría de melón

1 kg (2 lb 3 oz) honeydew melon (about 1½ melons), thickly peeled, seeds removed

zest of ½ lime

juice of 1 lime

salt flakes and ground white pepper

8 thin slices of jamón

bunch of mint, leaves picked, plus extra to serve

iced water

60 ml (¼ cup) light-tasting extra virgin olive oil

Preheat the oven to 180°C (350°F) fan-forced. Line a baking tray with baking paper.

Slice a thin wedge off the melon and cut the flesh into small dice. Set aside. Blend the remaining melon in a food processor with the lime zest and juice, adding salt and white pepper to taste. Add 125 ml (½ cup) of water and blend until smooth. Pour into a large jug and refrigerate.

Spread the jamón in a single layer on the prepared tray and bake for 12–15 minutes, until crisp.

Bring a small saucepan of water to the boil and blanch the mint leaves for 1 minute. Drain and refresh in iced water, then strain and squeeze out as much water as possible. Transfer the mint to a food processor, add the oil and blend on high until smooth.

Give the melon soup a good stir, then pour into serving bowls. Decorate with the jamón shards and diced melon, drizzle with the infused mint oil and garnish with mint leaves.

Mussels are economical and environmentally sustainable, as well as being an excellent source of protein, iron and omega 3s. Pairing these abundant molluscs with fresh chorizo perfectly encapsulates Spain's love of 'surf and turf'. I like to chargrill the tomatoes to take me back to the good times of campfires on the beach, eating mussels straight from the pot and scooping up all the goodness from the pan using the mussel shell as a shovel.

Mejillones con chorizo

4 roma (plum) tomatoes

1 tablespoon extra virgin olive oil

150 g (5½ oz) fresh chorizo sausage, de-cased

4 shallots, quartered

4 garlic cloves, chopped

2 sprigs of tarragon

250 ml (1 cup) dry white wine

125 ml (½ cup) dry sherry

1.5 kg (3 lb 5 oz) mussels, scrubbed and debearded

4 thick slices sourdough, chargrilled

Heat a barbecue grill plate to high. Add the tomatoes and char until the skins begins to blacken and shrink away from the flesh. Remove from the heat and, once cool enough to handle, remove and discard the skins and roughly chop the flesh into chunks. Set aside in a bowl.

Heat the olive oil and chorizo in a large saucepan or deep frying pan over high heat. Cook, stirring and breaking up the chorizo with a wooden spoon, for 5 minutes, until crispy. Add the shallot and cook for 5 minutes, then add the garlic and stir to combine. Add the chopped tomato, tarragon, white wine and sherry, then bring to the boil and cook for 8–10 minutes, until slightly reduced. Tip the mussels into the pan and stir to coat them in the sauce. Cover with a lid and steam, shaking the pan from side to side every so often, for 6–8 minutes, until the mussels have opened. Toss the mixture to lift up any chorizo that's gravitated to the bottom of the pan and discard any mussels that are still closed.

Serve the mussels in the pan at the table, with the chargrilled sourdough and plenty of serviettes and finger bowls.

If you fly into Barcelona's El Prat airport in late spring and catch the train through the Delta del Llobregat, you'll spot a purple sea of blooming perennial artichokes growing among the yellow flowering fennel. They're a big part of the local landscape no matter how much Barcelona sprawls, and they emit a calming, grounding vision after the hustle of the busy airport.

You can serve this dish as a side to a simple pan-fried fish fillet or roast chicken, as an entrée or as a star on its own with crusty bread and extra virgin olive oil.

Alcachofas a la Catalana

6–8 artichokes, hard outer leaves removed

iced water

2 lemons

1½ tablespoons extra virgin olive oil

1 thick slice speck, pancetta, or bacon, roughly chopped

¼ fennel bulb, sliced, fronds reserved

2 celery stalks, sliced into chunks

2 garlic cloves, smashed

1 fresh bay leaf

2 tablespoons raisins

80 ml (⅓ cup) dry sherry or white wine, plus extra if needed

200 g (7 oz) baby spinach leaves

1 tablespoon pine nuts, toasted

1 teaspoon salt flakes

Trim the artichoke stalks, leaving 4–5 cm (1¾–2 in) attached, then peel the outer layer of the stalks with a vegetable peeler. Cut the artichokes in half lengthways and remove the fibrous choke from the middle. Transfer to a large bowl filled with iced water and squeeze in the juice of ½ lemon.

Heat the olive oil in a large frying pan with a lid or a wide saucepan over medium–high heat. Add the speck, pancetta or bacon and fry until the fat has rendered and the pork is just beginning to crisp. Strain the artichokes and add to the pan, along with the fennel, celery and garlic, and lightly sauté for 2 minutes. Add the bay leaf and raisins and stir to combine, then add the sherry or white wine. Reduce the heat to medium–low, cover and cook for about 8 minutes, until the liquid has reduced by half. Remove the lid and squeeze in the juice of 1 lemon.

Continue cooking to reduce as much liquid as you like, making sure that the artichokes are soft and a knife slips through the stalks easily by the end of cooking (add more wine or water if necessary).

Remove from the heat and gently stir through the baby spinach leaves and the juice from the remaining lemon half. Transfer to a large serving platter and scatter the pine nuts, reserved fennel fronds and salt flakes over the top.

Island panzanella

Never mind about not eating your crusts – this is the salad of crusts! This refreshing dish from Formentera and Ibiza was traditionally made by fishermen using up the ends of leftover bread. The men would take the bread with them on long hauls at sea, where they would make this salad, along with some of the day's catch.

Day-old bread is best, but it's not imperative. If you do use stale bread, rehydrate it with a sprinkling of water before baking, to get it even drier and less chewy. This allows the bread to better absorb the vinaigrette, while keeping that crunchy texture alive.

Ensalada de crostes

450 g (1 lb) day-old crusty bread, ripped into bite-sized chunks

1 white onion, thinly sliced into rings

iced water

2½ tablespoons extra virgin olive oil, plus extra for drizzling

1½ tablespoons sherry vinegar

1 small green capsicum (bell pepper), very finely diced

2 garlic cloves, thinly sliced

small pinch of caster (superfine) sugar

500 g (1 lb 2 oz) mixed tomatoes, roughly chopped or sliced

salt flakes and freshly cracked black pepper

6 tinned sardines or large anchovy fillets

6 caper berries, halved

3 sprigs of parsley, roughly chopped

Preheat the oven to 180°C (350°F) fan-forced.

Place the bread on a baking tray in a single layer and lightly sprinkle with water (or use a spray bottle if you have one). Transfer to the oven and bake for 20 minutes or until lightly toasted and completely dry.

Meanwhile, place the onion in a bowl of iced water and set aside for 10 minutes.

Mix the olive oil, vinegar, capsicum, garlic and sugar in a small bowl to make a dressing.

Drain the onion and place in a mixing bowl with the toasted bread, tomato and dressing. Season with salt and pepper and toss well for 1 minute to combine, making sure the bread is completely coated in the dressing. Scatter over the sardines or anchovies, caper berries and parsley, and serve immediately.

Seafood paella broth

Many cuisines have a much-loved comforting, soupy rice dish and Spain is no exception. The quality of the fish stock is important in this dish, which makes this recipe slightly epic to make, but completely worth it. It's usually served with lobster, but only during spring and summer (due to catch limits); however, you will find this sophisticated seafood paella all year round at restaurants that have frozen some of the season's catch.

Arroz caldoso de marisco

2 tablespoons extra virgin olive oil

1 red capsicum (bell pepper), finely diced

300 g (10½ oz) firm white fish fillets, such as rock ling, cut into 2–3 cm (¾–1¼ in) chunks

1 onion, finely chopped

2 garlic cloves, minced

salt flakes

3 large tomatoes, grated, skins discarded

1 teaspoon smoked pimentón

100 g (3½ oz) calamari hoods, cleaned and diced

400 g (14 oz) short-grain rice, such as bomba or calasparra

2.5 litres (2.5 qts) Caldo de pescado (see page 262)

8 mussels, scrubbed and debearded

4 raw scampi

8 large raw prawns (shrimp), peeled and deveined

2 lemons, halved

Heat the oil in a 32–34 cm (12¾–13½ in) paella pan or large frying pan over medium heat. Add the capsicum and sauté for 8–10 minutes, until soft and the colour has leached out into the oil. Using a slotted spoon, remove the capsicum from the pan and set aside. Add the fish fillets to the pan and cook for 3 minutes each side until golden. Remove from the pan and set aside.

Next, add the onion, garlic and a pinch of salt to the pan and cook for 8–10 minutes, until completely soft. Add the tomato and pimentón, then reduce the heat to medium–low and cook, stirring frequently, for 15–20 minutes, until the liquid has all but evaporated. Add the calamari and cook for 5 minutes, then add the rice and stir to coat the grains. Pour in three-quarters of the stock and stir until the mixture comes to the boil. Reduce the heat to a gentle simmer and cook for 10–15 minutes, until the rice is cooked through.

Add the remaining stock to the pan and bring to the boil, then add the mussels, scampi, prawns and reserved fish fillets and capsicum. Reduce the heat to a gentle simmer and cook for 5 minutes or until the prawns are cooked through and the mussels have opened.

Serve the paella in the pan with the lemon halves for squeezing over.

Like French ratatouille, Spanish pisto and Catalan samfaina, the Balearic Islands have their own version of slow-cooked vegetables. With the addition of potato, the ingredients are roasted in the oven in this elegant version, which is humbly satisfying, especially when made with good-quality summer produce from the garden or local neighbourhood. Mallorcans serve this classic as an appetiser or in the centre of the table as an accompaniment to fish or meat. There is often no need for forks, as it just gets scooped up with a slice of local bread, bypassing even the plate. You might want to wear a bib if you want to experience it this way!

Tumbet de verduras

1 kg (2 lb 3 oz) ripe roma (plum) tomatoes, grated, skins discarded

salt flakes and freshly cracked black pepper

2 teaspoons dried oregano

3 fresh bay leaves

½ teaspoon caster (superfine) sugar

2 eggplants (aubergines), sliced into 2 cm (¾ in) thick rounds

2 teaspoons fine sea salt

250 ml (1 cup) extra virgin olive oil

400 g (14 oz) potatoes, peeled and sliced into 1.5 cm (½ in) thick rounds

1 large zucchini (courgette), sliced into 2 cm (¾ in) thick rounds

1 red capsicum (bell pepper), sliced into 2 cm (¾ in) thick rings

1 green capsicum (bell pepper), sliced into 2 cm (¾ in) thick rings

1 red onion, sliced into 2 cm (¾ in) thick rings

3 garlic cloves, thinly sliced

90 g (¼ cup) honey

80 g (2¾ oz) walnuts, chopped

Place the grated tomato in a fine sieve over a bowl to drain off some of the liquid. Transfer to a bowl, season with salt and pepper and mix through the oregano, bay leaves and sugar.

Place the eggplant in a large colander with a bowl underneath and sprinkle over the fine sea salt. Set aside for 6–8 minutes, to draw out the eggplant's bitter juices. Rinse off the salt and squeeze the slices dry with a clean tea towel, removing as much moisture as possible.

Heat the olive oil in a large heavy-based frying pan over medium heat. Add the potato and cook each side for 8–12 minutes, until golden and cooked through. Transfer to a large plate lined with paper towel to absorb the excess oil. Repeat this process for each vegetable, cooking the eggplant and zucchini for 5–7 minutes each side and the capsicum and onion for 3–5 minutes each side.

In the same pan, fry the grated tomato for 6–8 minutes, until starting to darken in colour.

Preheat the oven to 180°C (350°F) fan-forced.

Spoon a layer of the tomato sauce in the base of a large earthenware baking dish and top with half the garlic. Cover with a layer of potato, followed by the zucchini, capsicum, onion and finally the eggplant, seasoning with salt and pepper between each layer. Spoon over the remaining tomato sauce and garlic and tuck the bay leaves in between the vegetables. Drizzle over the honey.

Transfer the dish to the oven and roast for 30 minutes or until you see the juices starting to bubble. Throw the walnuts on top and return to the oven for 10 minutes to toast them slightly.

Serve the vegetables on their own or as part of a spread to accompany whatever you like. This dish goes particularly well with fish, lamb or even big spoonfuls of fresh ricotta.

In this one-dish wonder, fish fillets lie blanketed between delicate potato, spinach and tomato and sprinkled with pine nuts and raisins. Small whole fish are also sometimes used and I like to think the tomatoes on top were originally placed to mark the location of the fish underneath, so when it came to serving everyone would get their portion of fish in one piece. I like to add lots of tomato, as I find the liquid soaks right down to the potatoes, helping to keep the dish moist. It might not be so easy to locate the fish, though!

Cazuela de pescado al horno

bunch of English spinach, thick stems discarded, roughly chopped

2 teaspoons salt flakes

60 ml (¼ cup) extra virgin olive oil

500 g (1 lb 2 oz) desiree potatoes, peeled and thinly sliced

1 teaspoon sweet pimentón

bunch of spring onions (scallions), sliced

bunch of parsley, roughly chopped

3 garlic cloves, finely chopped

½ teaspoon ground cinnamon

freshly cracked black pepper

6 x 150 g (5½ oz) firm white fish fillets, such as snapper or hake

30 g (1 oz) pine nuts

50 g (1¾ oz) raisins

3–4 very ripe heirloom tomatoes, sliced

125 ml (½ cup) dry white wine

lemon wedges, to serve (optional)

Preheat the oven to 180°C (350°F) fan-forced.

Place the spinach in a large colander over a bowl, sprinkle with 1 teaspoon of the salt and set aside for 20 minutes.

Pour 2 tablespoons of the olive oil into a large round earthenware dish or baking dish and layer the potato slices on top. Sprinkle with ½ teaspoon of the remaining salt and the pimentón.

Squeeze out as much liquid as possible from the spinach, then transfer to a large bowl and add the spring onion, parsley, garlic and cinnamon. Toss to combine, then spread half the spinach mixture over the potato and press down with your hands to flatten the layers.

Sprinkle the remaining salt and a little pepper over both sides of the fish fillets and place on top of the spinach layer. Top with the remaining spinach mixture, sprinkle over the pine nuts and raisins and finish with the tomato. Pour over the wine and drizzle with the remaining olive oil, then season again with salt and pepper.

Make a cartouche by cutting a circle of baking paper 2 cm (¾ in) wider than your dish. Tuck it into the dish to create a loose seal, then transfer to middle shelf of the oven and bake for 20 minutes. Remove the cartouche and continue to cook for a further 30–40 minutes, until the tomato begins to colour and the potato is cooked through.

Divide into portions, trying to remember where each fish fillet is, and serve with lemon wedges on the side, if you like.

Stuffed vegetables are iconic throughout the Mediterranean. From Cyprus in the east and the neighbouring Aegean Islands, to Malta, Corsica, Sardinia and, of course, Spain, they all have a signature recipe for hulling out various whole vegetables and stuffing them with an array of delectable ingredients. As a point of difference from its Mediterranean cousins, this classic Spanish version uses chorizo and fennel.

Verduras rellenas

2 potatoes, halved

2 zucchini (courgettes), halved lengthways

2 long thin eggplants (aubergines), halved lengthways

2½ tablespoons extra virgin olive oil

1 onion, finely diced

2 garlic cloves, finely chopped

1 teaspoon fennel seeds

1 teaspoon allspice

1 teaspoon finely chopped rosemary leaves

150 g (5½ oz) lean minced (ground) pork

250 g (9 oz) lean minced (ground) beef

100 g (3½ oz) fresh chorizo sausage, de-cased

salt flakes

3 sprigs of marjoram or oregano, leaves picked and chopped

freshly cracked black pepper

250 g (1 cup) passata (puréed tomatoes)

2 slices of fresh bread, blitzed in a food processor

Preheat the oven to 200°C (400°F) fan-forced. Line a deep baking dish with baking paper.

Place the potato in a large saucepan of salted water and bring to the boil. Cook for 4 minutes, then drain and set aside until cool enough to handle. Scoop out the potato flesh, leaving a 1 cm (½ in) layer of potato around the edges and base. Discard the potato flesh or save for another use.

Spoon out the zucchini and eggplant flesh in the same way, then finely chop the flesh and set aside.

Heat the olive oil in a large heavy-based saucepan over medium–high heat. Add the onion and garlic and cook, stirring frequently, for 10 minutes or until soft and golden. Stir through the fennel seeds, allspice and rosemary leaves and cook for 2 minutes. Add the minced pork, beef and chorizo, along with a pinch of salt and the chopped zucchini and eggplant, and cook, breaking up any lumps with the back of a wooden spoon, for 10 minutes or until the meat has browned and any liquid has evaporated.

Transfer the mixture to a large bowl and set aside to cool a little before adding the marjoram or oregano and seasoning with salt and pepper.

Spoon the mixture into the hollowed-out vegetables and place in the prepared dish.

Spoon 1–2 tablespoons of the passata over the top of each stuffed vegetable half, then sprinkle over the breadcrumbs and bake for 10–12 minutes, until golden.

This dish involves toasting short-cut spaghetti, before combining with a sofrito base and adding flavours of the sea. Although called a paella, its cooking technique more closely resembles that of a pilaf. It is said to have been invented at sea by fishermen who had run out of rice and substituted the short, thin noodles picked up over the Mediterranean Sea in Corsica or Sardinia. Brought onto shore where Catalonia borders Valencia, the region is now home to this classic dish that mimics all the rich shellfish contents of the famous Valencian seafood paella.

Fideuá de sepia y gambas

300 g (10½ oz) fideos, angel hair short-cut pasta or spaghettini, cut into 5 cm (2 in) lengths

60 ml (¼ cup) extra virgin olive oil

2 garlic cloves, smashed

1 red capsicum (bell pepper), cut into short thin strips

1 litre (4 cups) Caldo de pescado (see page 262) or store-bought fish stock

1 fresh bay leaf

pinch of saffron threads

1 teaspoon salt flakes

280 g (1 cup) Sofrito (see page 258)

300 g (10½ oz) whole cuttlefish or calamari, cleaned and rinsed, hoods finely diced (or minced in a blender), tentacles set aside

150 g (5½ oz) small peeled prawns (shrimp)

8 large raw prawns (shrimp)

Alioli (see page 256), to serve

lemon wedges, to serve

Toast the fideos with 2 tablespoons of the olive oil and one garlic clove in a 32–34 cm (12½–13¼ in) paella pan or ovenproof frying pan over medium–high heat. Keep moving the pasta around the pan with a wooden spoon or spatula for 8–12 minutes, until evenly toasted and golden. Transfer to a large plate in a single layer and set aside.

Reduce the heat to medium, add the remaining oil and the capsicum to the pan and cook, stirring occasionally, for 8–10 minutes, until soft and the red of the capsicum has leached out into the oil. Transfer the capsicum to a small plate.

Meanwhile, heat the fish stock, bay leaf, saffron and salt in a saucepan over medium heat until simmering.

Preheat the oven to 180°C (350°F) fan-forced.

Add the sofrito to the pan and heat until sizzling, then add the finely diced cuttlefish or calamari. Cook for 5 minutes, add the small prawns and stir through for 2 minutes, then add the toasted fideos. Stir to coat well, then add the cuttlefish or calamari tentacles and the warmed stock and shake the pan gently to evenly distribute the fideos.

Reduce the heat to low and simmer for 10 minutes, until three-quarters of the liquid has evaporated. Place the large prawns and reserved capsicum on top, then transfer the pan to the oven for 12 minutes and watch the fideos spike up towards the heat!

Serve with alioli and lemon wedges.

The wild, forest alpine strawberries *fresas del bosque* are prized by pastry chefs and speciality fruit suppliers throughout Europe for their prettiness and superior fragrance and flavour. Similar in size and shape to a small raspberry, they make for very decorative arrangements on top of cakes and slices. Here, the humble seasonal field strawberry will do.

A quick and simple but sophisticated combination, you'll find this dessert on menus in cosmopolitan parts of the country, often served with a vanilla panna cotta, ice cream, almond cream or simply on their own to cleanse the palate after a long lunch.

Fresas con pimienta y balsamico

500 g (1 lb 2 oz) strawberries, hulled, larger ones halved

3 tablespoons pure icing (confectioners') sugar, plus extra to serve

1½ tablespoons aged balsamic vinegar

2 teaspoons black peppercorns, crushed in a mortar and pestle, or to taste

2 teaspoons pink peppercorns

Sprinkle the strawberries with the icing sugar and balsamic vinegar in a large bowl. Add the black pepper and allow to sit for 10 minutes.

Transfer to a serving bowl and scatter over the pink peppercorns. Sift a little extra icing sugar over the top and serve.

Fresh fruit is commonly served for dessert throughout Spain, and while the name obviously indicates this dish is not of Spanish origin, the Macedonian fruit salad is enjoyed throughout Europe, Argentina and Latin American countries where it is even sold in tins.

Indicative of the ethnic diversity of Alexander the Great's empire, this medley of fruit brings together a wide range of colours, flavours, textures and shapes.

Macedonia de frutas

¼ honeydew melon, peeled, seeds removed

¼ watermelon, peeled, seeds removed

1 pomegranate, arils removed

¼ pineapple, peeled, cored and diced

200 g (7 oz) mixed berries

1 kiwi fruit, diced

1 mandarin, segmented

2 figs, quartered

juice of 1 orange

zest and juice of 1 lime

2 teaspoons pure icing (confectioners') sugar

mint leaves, to garnish

edible flowers, to garnish (optional)

Use a melon baller to scoop out balls from the honeydew melon and watermelon. Transfer to a large bowl, add the remaining ingredients and stir well to combine.

Serve in bowls, garnished with fresh mint leaves and edible flowers, if desired.

The Spanish may like to go all out when it comes to cooking on the weekend, but during the working week evening meals are usually a simple affair, often consisting of a protein paired with vegetables or a salad, and perhaps finished with a piece of fruit.

The meal is enjoyed later in the day than other European countries, as a result of the traditional afternoon *siesta* and later morning starts that still dictate the daily routine of Spanish life. Most children also have after-school activities before spending the early-evening hours playing outside (few families have the luxury of a backyard) and coming home for dinner, tired and hungry.

The recipes in this chapter reflect this Iberian approach to midweek simplicity, with meals that are either quick to make or can be left to simmer on the stove while you wind down after a day's work. For a Spanish tortilla with a difference, the mushroom and silverbeet (Swiss chard) omelette can be made in less than 20 minutes using few ingredients. Pair with crusty bread for a speedy dinner with a complex flavour.

Pan-fried or oven-roasted fish also comes together quickly, and can be served with a salad or vegetables depending on the season or what you have on hand. When cherries are at their best, try the roasted duck for bit of midweek luxury. Served with a glass of Spanish red, it's the perfect meal for when friends or family drop by for a catch-up. And for the cooler months, stove-top stews, such as the lamb ragout and braised pork, bring warmth and comfort; you don't have to plan or prep too hard, simply throw everything in the pot and let the ingredients do the work for you.

This Spanish minestrone is traditionally made with fresh legumes, rather than dried. In winter, you might find pumpkin and potato in place of out-of-season beans, but come early spring the markets are bursting with fresh produce such as broad (fava) beans, borlotti (cranberry) beans, peas and runner (flat) beans. Each region adds their own locally cured meats to the soup, too, such as black or white pudding or thick slices of pancetta.

Sopa de minestra

2 tomatoes

iced water

1½ tablespoons extra virgin olive oil

150 g (5½ oz) pancetta or streaky bacon, finely chopped

4 spring onions (scallions), finely chopped

3 garlic cloves, finely chopped

6 Dutch carrots, sliced into 1.5 cm (½ in) thick rounds

1 celery stalk, cut into 1.5 cm (½ in) dice

½ fennel bulb, cut into 1.5 cm (½ in) dice

4 sprigs of marjoram or oregano

1 strip of lemon peel, white pith removed

2 fresh bay leaves

1 litre (4 cups) vegetable or chicken stock

100 g (3½ oz) runner (flat) beans, trimmed and cut into 4 cm (1½ in) lengths

80 g (½ cup) frozen peas

100 g (3½ oz) frozen broad (fava) beans, thawed and double-podded

salt flakes and freshly cracked black pepper

½ bunch of chives, finely snipped

Using a sharp knife, score a cross in the base of the tomatoes. Bring a saucepan of water to the boil and blanch the tomatoes for 2 minutes or until the skins start to curl away from the flesh. Immediately drain and plunge into iced water, then peel away the skins and cut the flesh into quarters. Remove and discard the seeds, then cut the quarters in half and set aside.

Heat the olive oil in a large saucepan over medium–high heat. Add the pancetta and cook for 4–5 minutes, until golden brown, then add the spring onion and garlic and cook, stirring, for 3–4 minutes, until the spring onion has softened. Add the chopped tomato and cook, stirring, for 2 minutes, then reduce the heat to medium–low and add the carrot, celery, fennel, marjoram or oregano, lemon peel and bay leaves. Cook, stirring occasionally, for 8–10 minutes, until the vegetables are soft but not caramelised.

Pour in the stock, cover with a lid and increase the heat to high. Remove the lid as soon as the mixture starts to boil and add the beans, peas and broad beans. Simmer for 4–6 minutes, until the beans are cooked through, then remove from the heat and season to taste with salt and pepper.

Ladle the minestrone into serving bowls and serve, garnished with the chives.

Foraging for mushrooms is a popular tradition in Spain where there are more than one hundred edible varieties. The most common mushrooms served on menus and sold in markets at the beginning of autumn are white saddle, black trompettes, coral mushrooms and the *l'esclata-sang* or red pine mushroom.

The combination of egg, mushroom and silverbeet in this recipe is soulful, earthy and grounding. Feel free to mix up the mushrooms with whatever is available at your local market, but do try and use different colours and textures.

Tortilla de setas y acelgas

2 teaspoons butter

1 tablespoon extra virgin olive oil

1 salad onion, sliced

400 g (14 oz) mixed mushrooms, roughly chopped

2 garlic cloves, finely chopped

1 sprig of thyme

125 ml (½ cup) dry sherry or dry white wine

8 silverbeet (Swiss chard) leaves, stalks removed, larger leaves cut in half

8 large eggs, lightly beaten

crusty bread, to serve

Heat the butter and olive oil in a large heavy-based frying pan over medium–high heat. Add the onion and cook for 4–6 minutes, until translucent and starting to soften. Add the mushroom, garlic, thyme and sherry or white wine, then increase the heat to high and cook, stirring constantly, for 6–8 minutes, until the mushroom is golden and tender.

Add the silverbeet leaves and pour in the beaten egg. Reduce the heat to low and stir until the egg starts to scramble. Using a spatula, evenly distribute the egg throughout the mushroom and silverbeet mixture, then cover with a lid and cook for 3–4 minutes, until the egg is cooked and golden on the base, but still quite moist in the middle.

Serve with a big chunk of crusty bread.

Cauliflower braise

Originating from Mallorca, this braise uses a distinct cooking technique where the ingredients sweat and cook in a large, tightly sealed stockpot that creates a gentle pressure from the locked-in steam and fat. As the ingredients cook, you shake the pot from side to side to mix the contents, all the while retaining the steam and avoiding mashing up the ingredients.

Traditionally, this dish is served with sliced black pudding on the side, but it's equally delicious on its own.

Coliflor rehogada

2 tomatoes

iced water

1½ tablespoons extra virgin olive oil

150 g (5½ oz) pancetta or streaky bacon, roughly chopped

2 teaspoons aniseed or fennel seeds

4–5 spring onions (scallions), chopped

3 garlic cloves, finely chopped

1 head of cauliflower, cut into small florets

1 teaspoon sweet pimentón, plus extra for dusting

30 g (¼ cup) raisins, roughly chopped

30 g (1 oz) pine nuts, toasted

salt flakes and freshly cracked black pepper

chopped parsley leaves, to serve

Using a sharp knife, score a cross in the base of the tomatoes. Bring a saucepan of water to the boil and blanch the tomatoes for 2 minutes or until the skins start to curl away from the flesh. Immediately drain and plunge into iced water, then peel away the skins and cut the flesh into quarters. Remove and discard the seeds, then finely dice the flesh and set aside.

Heat the olive oil in a large stockpot over medium–high heat. Add the pancetta and cook for 4–5 minutes, until golden, then add the aniseed or fennel seeds, spring onion and garlic and cook, stirring, for 3–4 minutes, until the spring onion has softened. Stir through the chopped tomato and cook for 2 minutes, then reduce the heat to medium–low, add the cauliflower, pimentón, raisins and pine nuts and stir well to combine.

To create a tight seal for your pot, wrap the lid in at least one thick tea towel. Cover the pot with the wrapped lid and cook for 5 minutes. Shake the pot from time to time, holding the lid tightly as you slide the pan back and forth over the burner. Open the lid to check if the ingredients are catching on the bottom and reduce the heat if so. Replace the lid and continue cooking for a further 15 minutes, carefully shaking the pot every 3 or so minutes.

Transfer the braised cauliflower to a serving dish, season to taste with salt and pepper and serve with a few chopped parsley leaves sprinkled over the top.

This dish evokes the artistic style of architect and innovator Antoni Gaudí's broken ceramic tile mosaics. Its inspiration is a romantic nod to another important Catalan craftsman, the great chef Ferran Adrià, who has also made an innovative, modernist, ground-breaking career by using influences from nature, new techniques and history to produce enchanting and decorative creations. Gaudí red mullet first appeared in 1987 in Adrià's first cookbook *El Bulli: El sabor del Mediterráneo*, and it went on to make regular appearances on his menu at El Bulli until the restaurant closed 25 years later.

This version doesn't involve the molecular gastronomy applied to the original, but the visual senses and common connection between these two great contributors to Catalan culture are colourfully present for all to see.

Salmonete de Gaudí

4 x 100 g (3½ oz) red mullet or pink snapper fillets, skin on, pin-boned

1½ tablespoons extra virgin olive oil

⅓ red capsicum (bell pepper), finely diced

⅓ yellow capsicum (bell pepper), finely diced

1 small zucchini (courgette), finely diced

½ white onion, finely diced

1 tomato, finely diced

⅓ bunch of chives, finely chopped

salt flakes and freshly cracked black pepper

salad leaves, to serve

Preheat a grill (broiler) to medium–high. Cut out four squares of baking paper just larger than the fish fillets.

Brush the fish skin with a little of the olive oil and place each fillet on a square of baking paper.

Combine the capsicums, zucchini, onion, tomato and chives in a small bowl and season to taste. Evenly flatten the mixture onto the oiled fish skin.

Heat the remaining oil in a non-stick frying pan over high heat and gently slide each fillet off the paper into the pan, decorated side up. Cook for 2 minutes to seal the base of the fish, then carefully transfer the fish back to the baking paper squares and grill (broil) for 4–6 minutes, until lightly toasted.

Serve with salad leaves.

Cuttlefish is a spring catch with a mild and subtle flavour compared to its cephalopod relatives. Underrated in Western cooking, it's seen as very messy and difficult to handle due to its large ink sac and brown, slimy skin. But cooked low and slow, as it is here, the thick flesh melts in your mouth like a Manchego cheese, making it worth the effort.

Cuttlefish with peas is a much-loved dish throughout the Mediterranean, and Spain is no exception where it's very common to pair seafood with something seasonal from the vegetable patch. It's also often served with meatballs and potatoes, too.

Sepia con guisantes

700 g (1 lb 9 oz) cuttlefish, squid or calamari hoods, cleaned and cut into 4 cm (1½ in) pieces

1 teaspoon fine sea salt

1½ tablespoons extra virgin olive oil

100 g (3½ oz) pancetta, finely diced

1 white onion, roughly chopped

2 garlic cloves, smashed

salt flakes and freshly cracked black pepper

1 teaspoon sweet pimentón

125 ml (½ cup) dry white wine

3 tomatoes, grated, skins discarded

375 ml (1½ cups) Caldo de pescado (see page 262) or good-quality store-bought fish stock, plus extra if needed

300 g (10½ oz) fresh or frozen peas

parsley leaves, to serve

crusty bread or boiled potatoes, to serve (optional)

lemon wedges, to serve (optional)

Place the cuttlefish, squid or calamari in a large bowl and cover with plenty of cold water. Stir through the fine salt and set aside for 30 minutes. Drain and pat dry with paper towel.

Heat the olive oil in a large frying pan over medium heat and add the pancetta, onion and garlic, along with a pinch of salt and pepper. Gently sauté for 10–15 minutes, until the onion is soft and lightly coloured. Stir through the pimentón, then add the wine and cook until evaporated. Increase the heat slightly, add the tomato and simmer quite vigorously until the tomato and onion have reduced to a paste. Stir through the cuttlefish and cook until it turns opaque, then pour in the fish stock, reduce the heat and partially cover with a lid. Simmer gently for 40–50 minutes, until the cuttlefish is extremely soft and tender. If the cuttlefish still has some resistance, add a little more stock and continue to cook until soft.

Check the seasoning and adjust if necessary, then add the peas and cook, uncovered, for 15 minutes if using fresh peas or 8 minutes if using frozen.

Divide the cuttlefish and peas among plates and top with a few parsley leaves. Serve with chunks of crusty bread or boiled potatoes and lemon wedges on the side, if you like.

Originating from the classic *tortilla española* (Spanish tortilla), this version dares to simplify and modernise it for the home cook, so that even a teenager can be bothered attempting it. A Ferran Adrià invention, he turned Spain's favourite tortilla into a unique 'hack' version that has now spread globally.

Tortilla de patatas 'chips'

1 tablespoon extra virgin
    olive oil

1½ onions, finely diced

¼ teaspoon salt flakes

6 large eggs

60 ml (¼ cup) full-cream (whole)
    milk

170 g (6 oz) good-quality salted
    potato chips (crisps)

Pan con tomate (see page 40),
    to serve

Heat half the olive oil in a small–medium non-stick frying pan over low heat. Add the onion and salt and sweat for 15 minutes, until completely soft and starting to colour. Remove from the heat and allow to cool.

Meanwhile, beat the eggs and milk in a bowl. Tip the potato chips into the egg mixture to soak, completely covering every chip. Set aside for 10 minutes.

Return the pan with the onion to medium heat, add a drizzle more oil and pour in the egg mixture, stirring to help the egg begin to cook. When the egg just starts to scramble, turn the heat to low and flatten the mixture with a spatula, smoothing out the top and around the edge of the pan. Shake the pan slightly and when the bottom of the egg has set, place a large dinner plate over the top and, using a tea towel to grip the frying pan handle, flip the tortilla over onto the plate. Add the remaining oil to the pan and slide the tortilla back into the pan. Tuck in the sides with the spatula and cook for another 2–3 minutes. Turn off the heat and cover with the dinner plate and allow to rest for a few minutes.

Turn the tortilla out onto a plate and serve with the pan con tomate.

There are many Mediterranean dishes that combine seafood and tomatoes, and in this recipe these best friends come together to make a restaurant-quality meal that's fresh, light and thoroughly delicious. Sometimes the simple things are the best!

Other sustainable fish, such as sea bass, bream or even barramundi, are also great in this dish.

Pargo con tomate corazón de buey

200 g (7 oz) oxheart or other large heirloom tomatoes, sliced into 2 cm (¾ in) thick rounds

200 g (7 oz) vine-ripened tomatoes, sliced into 2 cm (¾ in) thick rounds

2 teaspoons salt flakes

1 garlic clove, thinly sliced

1 x 650 g (1 lb 7 oz) snapper fillet, skin on

2 tablespoons extra virgin olive oil

1½ tablespoons sherry vinegar

40 g (⅓ cup) pitted black olives

½ celery heart, thinly sliced, leaves reserved

freshly cracked black pepper

2 limes, halved

Place the tomatoes in a bowl and sprinkle over half the salt. Mix through the garlic and set aside to macerate for 20 minutes.

Sprinkle the fish with the remaining salt and set aside in a large colander in the sink for 30 minutes.

Wipe the salt off the fish using paper towel and pat dry as much as you can. Set aside for a further 10 minutes, skin side up, to air-dry some more.

Meanwhile, finish the salad by combining half the oil, the vinegar, olives and celery with the tomatoes.

Heat a large frying pan over high heat. Rub the fish well with the remaining oil and gently place, skin side down, in the pan. Place a piece of baking paper followed by a weight, such as a small frying pan, on top of the fish to press the skin flush against the hot pan. Cook for 2–3 minutes, then use a spatula to gently lift a corner of the fish to check that it's not burning (reduce the heat if it is). Keep checking the underside of the fish until it is evenly golden, then flip over and cook for a further 2–3 minutes, depending on the thickness of your fish. You don't want to compress this side, as you may jeopardise the crispness of the skin.

Serve the fish with the tomato salad, a sprinkle of salt flakes and black pepper and the lime halves on the side.

A Balearic Christmas Day is a traditional family feasting event, unlike in the rest of Spain where families come together on Christmas Eve. It's a time for stuffing: stockings, pastas, animals and pastries! The first course is usually *sopa rellena*, a stock-based broth with stuffed large pasta shells. Then you may see either suckling pig, or roast turkey or chicken with a traditional stuffing, such as this recipe.

Pollo relleno con chorizo

1 x 1.8 kg (4 lb) free-range chicken, rinsed

100 ml (3½ fl oz) grape juice (mosto) or verjuice

100 ml (3½ fl oz) sherry vinegar

100 ml (3½ fl oz) vi ranci or port

2 teaspoons chopped marjoram or oregano leaves

salt flakes and freshly cracked black pepper

2 tablespoons extra virgin olive oil

1 large onion, finely diced

4 garlic cloves, minced

1 fresh bay leaf

1 fresh chorizo sausage, de-cased

200 g (7 oz) pork and fennel sausages, de-cased

30 g (¼ cup) raisins

90 g (3 oz) black grapes, quartered

50 g (1¾ oz) freshly blitzed breadcrumbs

20 g (¾ oz) slivered almonds, toasted

½ teaspoon ground cinnamon

1 tablespoon chopped tarragon leaves

20 g (¾ oz) good-quality lard or butter

1 teaspoon honey

Pat the chicken dry, then transfer to a wire rack, breast side up, set over a roasting tin and set aside in the fridge.

Make a basting dressing in a bowl with the grape juice, vinegar, vi ranci or port and marjoram or oregano. Season with salt and pepper and set aside.

To make the stuffing, heat the oil in a frying pan over medium heat. Add the onion, garlic and bay leaf and cook for 12–15 minutes, until the onion is golden. Increase the heat to high and add the chorizo, then stir through the sausage meat and cook, stirring, for 3–4 minutes. Transfer to a large bowl, add the raisins, grapes, breadcrumbs, almonds, cinnamon and tarragon and season with salt and pepper. Discard the bay leaf.

Preheat the oven to 180°C (350°F) fan-forced. Remove the chicken from the fridge.

Tightly roll three-quarters of the stuffing into three large balls, then pack each ball into the chicken. Wrap the remaining stuffing in baking paper and a layer of foil.

Rub the lard all over the chicken and pour half the basting dressing into the roasting tin with 250 ml (1 cup) water. Roast for 45 minutes, then remove the tin and turn over the chicken. Give the liquid in the tin a stir and puncture a few holes into the chicken with a kitchen skewer. Baste the top of the chicken with 2 tablespoons of the dressing, then return to the oven with the remaining stuffing and roast for another 30 minutes.

Increase the temperature to 220°C (430°F) and remove the tin again. Turn the chicken back over and pierce a few more holes on each side of the spine. Baste with another 2 tablespoons of dressing and add a little more water to the tin if the liquid is drying out. Roast for another 8–10 minutes, until the skin is golden and crisp. Turn the oven off, open the door to let the heat out and leave the chicken to rest for 12–15 minutes.

Combine any remaining pan juices in a jug with the last of the dressing and the honey. Serve the chicken with the dressing and extra stuffing on the side.

A simple yet sophisticated dish, perfect for special occasions when you don't want to spend hours fussing in the kitchen. Years ago, confit duck legs were only available in tins or from specialty markets, but nowadays farmed duck is readily available in restaurant-style cuts for convenience and sold at reasonable prices. Give this recipe a try with a buttery mashed potato or crispy dauphinoise the next time you're celebrating an anniversary or intimate birthday dinner.

Magret de pato con cerezas al horno

1 tablespoon extra virgin olive oil

4 bone-in duck breasts, skin scored

500 g (1 lb 2 oz) fresh or frozen cherries, pitted

40 g (1½ oz) butter, melted

1 tablespoon sherry vinegar

zest and juice of ½ orange

2 tablespoons brown sugar

1 teaspoon salt flakes

½ teaspoon ground white pepper

Preheat the oven to 200°C (400°F) fan-forced.

Heat half the oil in a large heavy-based frying pan and place the duck breasts, skin side down, in the pan. Cook for 4–6 minutes, until the skin is golden and blistering, then turn over and cook for a further 2–3 minutes, until golden. Transfer to a wire rack, skin side up, with a roasting tin underneath.

In a large bowl, toss the cherries with the butter, vinegar, orange zest and juice, sugar, salt and pepper. Transfer to a large baking dish and roast for 10 minutes.

At the same time, place the duck and the roasting tin in the oven and cook for 10–15 minutes, until cooked through to your liking, then remove and set aside to rest for 6–8 minutes.

Slice the duck breasts into three pieces and serve on a bed of the roasted cherries.

Braised pork & broad beans

Broad (fava) beans are a popular vegetable throughout Spain. The sweet and earthy baby beans are used in salads or pickled, while any larger pods that have spent too long on the plant are stewed, such as this meaty mountain dish.

Here, I use broad beans at three stages in their life cycle: unpodded broad beans to give earthiness and a thick texture; single-podded beans for a bitter creaminess; and naked green beans, which provide a nutty freshness.

Chuleta de cerdo con habas rehogadas

1 kg (2 lb 3 oz) fresh broad (fava) beans

2 teaspoons butter

60 ml (¼ cup) extra virgin olive oil

4 x 200 g (7 oz) pork chops

100 g (3½ oz) pancetta, cut into 1.5 cm (½ in) dice

1 onion, thinly sliced

1 tablespoon sobrassada (see page 8)

3 garlic cloves, finely chopped

150 ml (5 fl oz) dry sherry or dry white wine

800 ml (27 fl oz) chicken stock

zest and juice of 1 lemon

2 sprigs of mint, leaves picked

sea salt flakes and freshly cracked black pepper

crusty bread, to serve

Divide the broad beans into three even piles. Double-pod one-third of the beans, single-pod another third and leave the remaining beans whole, trimming any scraggy ends.

Heat the butter and half the olive oil in a large heavy-based frying pan over high heat. Add the pork chops and cook for 4–6 minutes until golden and sealed on both sides. Transfer to a wire rack with a roasting tin underneath and set aside.

In the same pan, cook the pancetta and onion over medium–high heat for 6–8 minutes, until the onion is soft and translucent. Add the sobrassada and garlic and cook for 3–4 minutes, until the sobrassada has melted.

Add the whole broad beans to the pan followed by the sherry or wine and bring to a simmer. Reduce the heat to medium and cook for 3–4 minutes, stirring the beans around to coat in the sauce.

Add the chicken stock and return the pork chops to the pan, along with the lemon zest. Cover with a tight-fitting lid and simmer for 12–15 minutes, until the beans are soft and wilted.

Stir through the single-podded beans and continue to simmer, covered, for another 8–10 minutes, until the skins begin to shrivel and shrink away from the beans. Increase the heat to high, add the final batch of beans and half the mint, and season with salt and pepper. Cook, uncovered, for 3–4 minutes, until the last batch of beans are just soft.

Divide the beans and pork chops among four serving plates, squeeze over the lemon juice and finish with the remaining mint leaves. Serve with crusty bread on the side.

Chunky lamb ragout

This slow-cooked lamb stew has French roots dating back to the revolutionary wars. Like the French *navarin printanier* (spring stew), except without the turnips and with the addition of pimentón, this dish requires little effort. You can make it the day before and have it ready to go the next day, or put it all in the slow cooker and forget about it.

Ragú de cordero

60 ml (¼ cup) extra virgin olive oil

3 garlic cloves, unpeeled, smashed

1 kg (2 lb 3 oz) boneless lamb shoulder, cut into 8 pieces

1 rack of lamb, cut into 4 double-rib cutlets

1½ onions, finely diced

1 large carrot, finely diced

8 French shallots, peeled

1 fresh bay leaf

2 sprigs of thyme

3 sprigs of marjoram or oregano

1 sprig of rosemary

1 teaspoon sweet pimentón

1 teaspoon ground coriander

1 teaspoon ground fennel

½ teaspoon ground white pepper

1 teaspoon salt flakes

1 tablespoon plain (all-purpose) flour

3 tomatoes, grated, skins discarded

1 tablespoon tomato paste (concentrated purée)

60 ml (¼ cup) Cognac

1 litre (4 cups) beef stock

bunch of Dutch carrots, peeled

155 g (1 cup) frozen peas

mashed potatoes, to serve

Heat half the olive oil and the garlic in a large heavy-based saucepan over medium–high heat. Add the lamb shoulder and cutlets and sear on all sides until golden. Transfer to a plate and set aside.

Reduce the heat to medium–low and add the remaining oil, the onion, carrot, shallots, herbs, spices, salt and flour. Sauté for 10 minutes or until soft and starting to colour.

Stir through the tomato and tomato paste and cook for 2 minutes, then add the Cognac, followed by the stock. Gently simmer, semi-covered, for 1 hour. Add the Dutch carrots and cook for a further 8–10 minutes, then stir through the peas in the final 5 minutes of cooking.

Serve with mashed potatoes.

Salads

Regardless of the season, there is a salad for every day of the year in Spain, such is the love for good-quality produce, simply prepared. Whether served as a seasonal accompaniment to the main meal or eaten as a stand-alone dish – perhaps for a light lunch or dinner when the summer evenings are too hot to contemplate standing over the stove – salads are a fundamental component of the Spanish cooking repertoire.

A Spanish salad can be as simple as tossing a few green leaves from the garden in a bowl, or a more complex meatier affair, such as *ensalada Catalana*, which boasts some of Catalonia's finest produce – namely *embutidos* (charcuterie) and white asaparagus.

Of course, with such good-quality produce available year-round, simplicity often wins the day. A classic tomato salad with locally grown Arbequina olives needs nothing more than a drizzle of extra virgin olive oil, a spritz of vinegar and a pinch of salt flakes. Or for something a little different, try the smashed onion salad with pickled cabbage – it's a brilliant way to incorporate winter veg into something light (especially served alongside heavy meat dishes), and its dramatic red-purple hue and pickled flavour will brighten the dreariest winter day.

While the salads may be varied, Spanish salad dressings will nearly always feature the same four ingredients: sherry vinegar, good-quality extra virgin olive oil, salt and pepper. If you visit someone's home in Spain, a salad will most likely be served undressed. The dressing ingredients will be in the middle of the table for you to help yourself and season your salad as you wish.

Feel free to swap any of the ingredients in the salads that follow – the Spanish have a flexible attitude towards produce, using what's in season and tastes the best, and so should you. As long as you remember the sherry vinegar, it will still be Spanish at heart.

Tomatoes are synonymous with Spain; there's even a yearly food-fight festival in Valencia province known as La Tomatina, where locals and visitors alike hurl the season's glut at each other for fun. It's certainly one way to deal with excess, fast-ripening tomatoes at the end of summer. Gazpacho, salmorejo and the versatile sofrito are other famous uses for this humble hero of Spanish cuisine. Make this salad when tomatoes are at their best towards the end of the season – locally sourced or homegrown tomatoes are even better – with really good-quality sherry vinegar.

Ensalada de tomate

1 white onion, sliced

iced water

400 g (14 oz) super-ripe heirloom tomatoes, roughly chopped or sliced

2 teaspoons salt flakes

2 tablespoons dried Greek or Mexican oregano

125 g (½ cup) Olivas Arbequinas (see page 16) or small wild olives

2 tablespoons good-quality sherry vinegar

60 ml (¼ cup) extra virgin olive oil

crusty bread, to serve

Plunge the onion into iced water and set aside for 5 minutes.

Arrange the tomato in a large serving dish and sprinkle over the salt flakes and oregano.

Drain the onion and scatter it over the tomato, along with the olives. Drizzle with the vinegar and olive oil.

Serve with crusty bread and a side of Sardines a la parilla (see page 214), if you like.

Broad (fava) beans are so hardy and easy to grow. In addition, they set up the vegetable garden for summer plantings by fixing much-needed nitrogen into the soil, paving the way for that sweet crop of tomatoes.

Inspiration for the flavour combinations in this dish comes from one of my favourite meals by chef Santi Santamaria, who unfortunately passed away too soon. The essence of fresh ginger paired with tiny-teeny bright-green freshly podded baby broad beans make this dish truly unforgettable.

Ensalada de habas y guisantes

500 ml (2 cups) vegetable stock

½ bunch of tarragon

200 g (7 oz) fresh or frozen podded baby broad (fava) beans

iced water

150 g (5½ oz) fresh or frozen podded peas

2 sprigs of mint, leaves picked and thinly sliced

salt flakes and freshly cracked black pepper

60 ml (¼ cup) extra virgin olive oil

1 tablespoon sherry vinegar

1 teaspoon freshly grated ginger

juice of ½ lemon

¼ radicchio, shredded

100 g (3½ oz) queso fresco or firm ricotta

Bring the vegetable stock and two sprigs of tarragon to the boil in a saucepan over medium–high heat.

Blanch the broad beans for 2 minutes then, using a slotted spoon, remove them from the stock and immediately transfer to a bowl of iced water. Remove the outer skins of most of the larger beans, leaving the smaller ones intact for a touch of bitterness.

Bring the stock back to the boil and blanch the peas for 4 minutes, then strain and cool in the iced water.

Finely chop the remaining tarragon leaves and place in a bowl, along with the blanched broad beans and peas, mint leaves, a pinch of salt and pepper and half the olive oil.

In a separate bowl, combine the vinegar, ginger, lemon juice and remaining oil, then toss through the shredded radicchio. Mix this through the broad bean and pea mixture.

Transfer the salad to a serving platter and dot the queso fresco or ricotta over the top.

Xató, from the word 'chateau' – refers to the size and decadence of this salad, which showcases the best produce from the Catalan region. It's so famous that it has its own festival – La ruta del Xató – which starts in the Garraf region, then moves inland to the wine region of El Penedès and down into the north of the Costa Daurada. Every town has its own variation of the salsa romesco and each claims the origin of this much-loved salad, traditionally eaten in Lent during the winter months.

The thick dip consistency of the salsa is hearty and wholesome and, paired with the bitterness of the greens, it never gets tired. It's Catalonia's version of hummus and crudités in a salad, but showcasing the sea.

Xatonada

150 g (5½ oz) bacalao (salt cod) fillets

1 frisée (curly endive), washed, dark green leaves discarded

150 g (5½ oz) tuna chunks in olive oil

4 salted anchovy fillets

2 tablespoons Arbequina olives or green manzanilla olives

280 g (1 cup) Salsa romesco (see page 261)

To prepare the bacalao, submerge the fish in cold water for 4–8 hours (depending on the thickness of the fish), changing the water every 2 hours. Tear the flesh away from any skin, bones and wings and taste for texture and saltiness. It should be soft with a hint of salt. If the bacalao is still too salty or dry, return it to fresh, clean water and change the water regularly until you've reached the desired texture and flavour.

Roughly tear any large frisée leaves, then remove any excess water with a clean tea towel and place the leaves on a large serving platter. Place the bacalao, tuna, anchovy fillets and olives on top of the frisée and finish with dollops of salsa romesco.

Catalan salad

You will find various permutations of this salad all over Spain, showcasing the best of Catalonian produce. No matter what the composition, what sets it apart from all the other Spanish table salads is the addition of *embutidos* (charcuterie).

This salad has a bit of everything and ticks most of the major food groups in one big bowl. It is almost always served with all the ingredients presented individually, including the oil, vinegar, salt and pepper, so you can dress the salad as you wish, and to keep the vinegar away from the cured meats. This version is more akin to a farmers'-style salad you may have found back in the day at an isolated mountain-side pit stop with a wild kitchen garden, but without all the homemade charcuterie offerings.

Ensalada Catalana

300 g (10½ oz) iceberg lettuce, roughly torn

2 vine-ripened tomatoes, cut into wedges

300 g (10½ oz) white asparagus from a jar or tin, rinsed and drained

400 g (14 oz) tin hearts of palm, rinsed and drained (optional)

1 carrot, shredded on a mandoline

4 radishes, thinly sliced

2 hard-boiled eggs, peeled and halved

4 cured chorizo, thinly sliced

4 slices of jamón or prosciutto

4 slices of salami

4 slices of mortadella, rolled up

8 green olives, stuffed with anchovy fillets

To serve

salt flakes and freshly cracked black pepper

sherry vinegar

good-quality extra virgin olive oil

Arrange all the salad ingredients decoratively in a bowl or on a serving platter in whichever order or design you prefer.

Serve in the centre of the table with the salt and pepper, vinegar and olive oil, so everyone can dress their own salad.

This salad is even better served with pan con tomate. (see page 40).

This dish, also called the Olivier salad after the Russian chef who invented it, appears in every Spanish canteen, on school-camp menus, at buffets, tapas bars and in the packaged food section of the supermarket. You can even buy the vegetables pre-cut, par-cooked and frozen, ready to reheat, dress and serve.

Waxy potatoes, such as nicola or kipfler (fingerling), are best for this salad, as they hold together well when cooked. The kipflers also cook quite evenly from the outside in because of their trunk-like shape. It's important to cook the vegetables whole to retain as much flavour as possible and to avoid too much water being absorbed.

Ensalada Rusa

1 kg (2 lb 3 oz) kipfler (fingerling) or nicola potatoes, scrubbed clean

2 small carrots or 4 Dutch carrots, scrubbed clean

2 eggs

80 g (½ cup) fresh or frozen green peas

iced water

salt flakes and ground white pepper

1 tablespoon sherry vinegar

1 tablespoon extra virgin olive oil

½ x quantity Mayonesa (see page 257)

185 g (6½ oz) tin good-quality tuna in olive oil

3 sprigs of curly parsley, leaves picked and chopped

Place the potatoes, carrots and eggs in a large saucepan and cover with water. Bring to the boil over medium–high heat, then reduce the heat to a simmer. Remove the eggs after 4 minutes and plunge into cold water. Peel the eggs as soon as they're cool enough to handle and roughly chop. The vegetables will take different times to cook, so keep an eye on them – you want them to be firm but not hard. When you can pierce them with a small knife or skewer with the slightest resistance, they are ready. Drain and set aside to cool a little.

Boil the peas in salted boiling water for 4–5 minutes if fresh, or 2 minutes if frozen. Drain and plunge into iced water to cool.

Peel the potatoes and carrots and cut into small chunks or cubes. Transfer to a large bowl, season with salt and white pepper and loosely dress with the vinegar and olive oil (the vegetables will better absorb the flavours when they are still warm). Allow to cool completely, then coat with the mayonesa and stir through the cooked peas, tuna and chopped egg.

Garnish with the curly parsley to keep things a little retro.

This simple, go-to warm salad is a modern favourite served in restaurants throughout the country. It's also very popular at big celebrations, where it's often served as an entrée.

The fats in the goat's cheese make it an ideal cheese to fry as you can get a crusty seal without the oils separating. Rinded goat's cheese is a French product and its soft, creamy and acidic flavour pairs perfectly here with the sweet vinaigrette and fresh bitter leaves.

Queso de cabra a la plancha

2 tablespoons raisins

60 ml (¼ cup) balsamic vinegar

1 teaspoon honey

80 ml (⅓ cup) extra virgin olive oil

3 tablespoons walnuts, toasted and chopped

½ teaspoon salt flakes

250 g (9 oz) goat's cheese log with rind, cut into 1–2 cm (½–¾ in) thick slices

freshly cracked black pepper

½ radicchio, leaves separated

70 g (2½ oz) rocket (arugula) leaves

1 red apple, cored and thinly sliced

½ bunch of chives, cut into 3 cm (1¼ in) lengths

Heat the raisins and balsamic vinegar in a small saucepan over medium heat and simmer for 4–5 minutes to rehydrate the raisins. Stir through the honey and remove from the heat. Allow to cool a little, then pour in the olive oil and add the walnuts and salt flakes. Set aside.

Line a baking tray with baking paper.

Heat a large non-stick frying pan over high heat. When the pan is extremely hot, add the goat's cheese slices and cook for 1–2 minutes each side. Transfer to the prepared tray and crack some black pepper over the top.

Arrange the salad leaves on serving plates and top with the apple and fried goat's cheese.

Spoon over the raisin dressing and rain over the chives.

The bourgeoisie of Spain have an obsession with foie gras – perhaps not quite as much as the French, but close. And lentils for that matter, too.

This cosmopolitan combination of decadence and benevolence follows a long tradition of pairing luxury ingredients with peasant produce to create a distinct level of refinement. The crusty, seared, salty foie gras next to the soft, earthy lentils and fresh, crunchy raw vegetables is a winning cocktail of textures, flavours and capitalism on one plate. Return this dish to its peasant roots, if you like, and use tinned tuna instead of foie gras, tinned lentils and whatever fresh vegetables are in season.

Ensalada de lentejas con foie gras

300 g (10½ oz) beluga lentils, soaked in 2 litres (68 fl oz) water overnight

1 fresh bay leaf

2 sprigs of thyme

1 garlic clove, minced

1½ teaspoons dijon mustard

juice of ½ lemon

1 tablespoon sherry or red wine vinegar

2½ tablespoons extra virgin olive oil

salt flakes and freshly cracked black pepper

1 carrot, finely diced

½ fennel bulb, finely diced

2 celery heart stalks, finely diced, leaves reserved for garnish

½ red onion, finely diced

3 radicchio leaves, roughly torn

2 tablespoons chopped chervil or flat-leaf parsley

⅓ bunch of chives, finely snipped

2 duck foie gras, sliced in half lengthways

Drain and rinse the lentils, then place in a large stockpot with more than enough water to fully cover them over medium heat. Add the bay leaf and thyme and bring to a simmer for 15 minutes, or until just tender but not falling apart. Remove from the heat and transfer the lentils and cooking liquid to a baking dish to cool a little. If they are really tender, skip this process and drain them straight away. Rinse them under cold water if they are already starting to fall apart – you will compromise some of the flavour but you won't be left with mushy lentils.

In a small bowl, make a dressing with the garlic, mustard, lemon juice, vinegar, 2 tablespoons of the olive oil and salt and pepper, to taste.

Once the lentils have cooled slightly, drain and toss with the dressing while still warm. Set aside to cool completely, then mix through the finely diced vegetables, radicchio and herbs.

Heat the remaining olive oil in a large frying pan over medium–high heat. Sear the foie gras for 1–2 minutes each side, then remove the pan from the heat and allow the foie gras to stand for another 1–2 minutes. It may still be slightly pink, but will continue to cook in the pan. Transfer to paper towel and season heavily with salt flakes.

Divide the lentils among bowls, top with the foie gras and reserved celery leaves and serve.

Mallorcan chopped salad

One of my all-time favourite salads, picked straight from the summer garden. The trick is to dice the vegetables evenly and small enough to fit one of every ingredient in your mouth at once. I add apple to my trampó, which isn't traditional but gives the salad a wonderfully tart freshness on a hot summer's day. Make sure you use the best cold-pressed extra virgin olive oil you can get your hands on.

Trampó

1 white onion, diced

iced water

1 granny smith apple, cored
    and diced

juice of ½ lemon

1 small green bullhorn pepper,
    diced

1 small red capsicum (bell
    pepper), diced

1 small yellow capsicum (bell
    pepper), diced

2 vine-ripened tomatoes, diced

2½ tablespoons extra virgin
    olive oil

1½ tablespoons sherry vinegar

1 teaspoon cumin seeds,
    toasted and ground

½ teaspoon sweet pimentón

salt flakes and freshly cracked
    black pepper

3 sprigs of marjoram or
    oregano, leaves picked

crusty bread, to serve

green olives, to serve (optional)

Place the white onion in a small bowl of iced water. Combine the apple and lemon juice in another bowl. Set both aside for 10 minutes, then drain.

Combine the pepper, capsicums, tomato, olive oil, vinegar, cumin and pimentón in a serving bowl, then add the onion and apple. Season with salt and pepper, to taste, and scatter over the marjoram or oregano leaves.

Serve with crusty bread and some green olives on the side, if you like.

Affectionately known as *la papa* in Spain (also the name for the Pope!), potatoes are hugely important in Iberian cuisine. As is mayonnaise, which the Spanish claim was stolen by the French from the Menorcan capital Mahon, during their occupation of the island and subsequently popularised by them around the world.

For this recipe, I like to leave the potato skins on for texture, colour and taste. Use as little or as much *mayonesa* as you like to dress the potatoes, and store the rest in an airtight container in the fridge for up to a week.

Patata I mayonesa

30 g (¼ cup) raisins, roughly chopped

2 tablespoons sherry vinegar

1 kg (2 lb 3 oz) baby (chat) potatoes

1 tablespoon extra virgin olive oil

1 salad onion, chopped

30 g (¼ cup) slivered almonds, toasted

6 sprigs of parsley, finely chopped

¼ bunch of dill, fronds picked and finely chopped

3 sprigs of tarragon, leaves picked, plus extra to serve

salt flakes and freshly cracked black pepper

Mayonesa (see page 257), to dress

Heat the raisins and sherry vinegar in a small saucepan over medium heat for 2–3 minutes. Set aside.

To make the mayonesa, place the egg yolk and egg in a mixing bowl or in the bowl of a food processor. Whisk or blitz to combine, then incorporate the vinegar, lemon juice and salt. Whisking or blitzing constantly, very gradually pour in the oils, one at a time, in a thin, steady stream, until you have a thick mayonnaise.

Place the potatoes in a large saucepan of salted water and bring to the boil. Cook for 25–30 minutes, until tender but not falling apart. Drain and transfer to a large bowl with the oil and vinegared raisins and their juice. Stir well to coat the potatoes, then set aside for 20 minutes or so before adding the remaining ingredients and mixing through as much mayonesa as you like. Sprinkle with a few extra tarragon leaves and serve.

This rich, wintery side salad makes a bold accompaniment for any meat or fish pate or terrine. With its dramatic flair, the deep, dark colours are reminiscent of dishes served up in the Baroque period, perhaps alongside a whole lamb and a *porron* of wine. I sometimes serve this with orange segments or wedges of pear, and some chargrilled slices of baguette drizzled with olive oil.

Cebolla rota con col escabechada

¼ red cabbage, cut into large, bite-sized chunks

1½ tablespoons fine sea salt

160 g (5½ oz) caster (superfine) sugar

250 ml (1 cup) white wine vinegar

1 fresh bay leaf

8 black peppercorns

4 allspice berries

6 pink onions, red salad onions or purple shallots, peeled

iced water

4–6 radishes, sliced

1½ tablespoons extra virgin olive oil

2 tablespoons micro herbs, such as sorrel or baby beetroot (beets) (optional)

Toss the cabbage in the salt and let stand for 30 minutes. Rinse well and completely dry with paper towel, then transfer to a large glass jar or non-reactive bowl.

Set aside 2 teaspoons of the sugar and tip the rest into a small saucepan. Add the vinegar, bay leaf, peppercorns, allspice and 60 ml (¼ cup) of water and bring to a simmer. Cook until the sugar is dissolved, then remove from the heat and set aside to cool. Once completely cool, pour over the cabbage and refrigerate.

Chop the onions into quarters or six chunks if really large. Place in a clean tea towel and, using a rolling pin or the base of a glass bottle, bruise the chunks to break them slightly and release some of their juice. Transfer to a bowl and sprinkle with the remaining sugar and a pinch of salt. Set aside for 5 minutes, then plunge into iced water and drain.

Remove two large handfuls of the cabbage from its pickling liquid (any left over can stay in the 'escabeche' and be used another time) and place in a bowl with the onion, radish and olive oil. Mix well to combine.

Divide the salad among plates and sprinkle with a few micro herbs, if desired.

sunday

Sessions

A hangover day for some, Sundays in Spain are an adjective, a vibe, a total mood. Typically, 'to *dominguero*' is to take a day trip, drive slowly around the countryside, laze about the house watching movies or have a quiet stroll along the beachfront. Although the day's activities may change depending on where you are and who you're with, the one thing that never alters is the time devoted to making and enjoying food.

This dedication to food rituals and eating is a constant in Spanish communities throughout the country. It might involve coming together in the kitchen to prepare beer snacks for the latest soccer game on TV, or baking a batch of empanadas and heading down the beach on a summer's day.

If you've got a few hours spare, try your hand at the lemon marmalade in this chapter. It makes a refreshing change to the regular orange variety and is wonderful spread on toast or croissants. Or if you want to cook a Sunday family lunch with a difference, break out the paella pan and make *arroz negro*. This stunning rice dish is oil-slick black from the squid ink, which contrasts the lashings of creamy *alioli* it's traditionally served with. It makes an impressive centrepiece to any Spanish home-cooked feast, requiring nothing more than crusty bread and a simple side salad to help feed the masses.

For true Spanish decadence, however, look no further than the classic Ibizan fish stew *bullit de pescado* with *arroz a banda* (rice on the side). The rice is cooked using the stock from the stew, resulting in a rich, deeply flavoured side dish that's just as filling as the main event.

If this all feels too much on your day of rest, then fire up the barbecue, hook up a chicken to a rotisserie and forget about it while you get on with your *siesta*. Whatever you choose, treat yourself to a Spanish-style Sunday: chill, drink, cook, eat, repeat!

Every country has a favourite pie and Spain is no exception. Distinguished by its filling and shape, these curious empanadas (meaning 'to wrap up') are individually 'sculpted' like clay, then filled and 'fired' in the oven. Although an unusual addition, the orange juice in the dough softens the richness of the lard.

Empanadas de cordero

100 g (3½ oz) lard or butter, at room temperature

60 ml (¼ cup) extra virgin olive oil, plus extra for greasing

180 ml (6 fl oz) freshly squeezed orange juice

pinch of fine sea salt

500 g (1 lb 2 oz) plain (all-purpose) flour, plus extra for dusting

Lamb filling

400 g (14 oz) boneless lamb shoulder, cut into 2 cm (¾ in) dice

120 g (4½ oz) sobrassada (see page 8)

120 g (4½ oz) pancetta, diced

1½ teaspoons smoked pimentón

1½ tablespoons extra-virgin olive oil

200 g (7 oz) frozen peas

salt flakes and freshly cracked black pepper

Place the lard or butter and olive oil in the bowl of a stand mixer with the whisk attached and beat until combined. Add the orange juice and fine sea salt and mix on medium speed for a few minutes to form a paste.

Swap the whisk for the dough hook attachment, add the flour and knead for 4–5 minutes on medium speed until a dough forms. Wrap tightly in plastic wrap and refrigerate for 15–20 minutes.

Meanwhile, combine the lamb filling ingredients, except the peas, in a bowl and season with salt and pepper. Set aside.

Preheat the oven to 160°C (320°F) fan-forced. Line two baking trays with baking paper.

Transfer the dough to a floured work surface and roll into a large log. Portion the dough into eight 55 g (2 oz) pieces (save the remaining dough for the pie lids). Working with one piece of dough at a time, roll the dough into a circle and use it to line the base and side of a small bowl with a 5 cm (2 in) base. Grease your fingers with a little oil if the dough is starting to stick. Carefully remove the moulded dough from the bowl and set aside on one of the prepared trays. Refrigerate while you prepare the pie lids.

Weigh out the remaining dough into eight 20 g (¾ oz) balls and roll each ball into a 6.5 cm (2½ in) circle.

Divide the filling evenly among the pie bases, leaving a 1–1.5 cm (½ in) gap at the top. Sprinkle the peas over the top and brush a little water around the edges. Drape the lids over the pie bases and pinch the dough together to seal.

Bake for 40–45 minutes, until golden and cooked through.

Set the pies aside on a wire rack to cool slightly and to allow the filling to continue cooking before serving.

Enjoy warm or at room temperature.

Originally from the Levant, these vegetarian savoury pasties are popular picnic fare throughout Spain. They're made with any combination of local seasonal vegetables, but they always include pine nuts and raisins, which are abundant throughout the peninsula.

Empanadas de verdura

100 g (3½ oz) lard or butter, at room temperature

60 ml (¼ cup) extra virgin olive oil, plus extra for greasing

180 ml (6 fl oz) freshly squeezed orange juice

pinch of fine sea salt

500 g (1 lb 2 oz) plain (all-purpose) flour, plus extra for dusting

Vegetable filling

300 g (10½ oz) silverbeet (Swiss chard), leaves stripped and finely chopped

200 g (7 oz) cauliflower florets, finely chopped

2 marinated artichoke hearts, finely chopped

1 tablespoon extra virgin olive oil

½ bunch of chives, finely chopped

2 tablespoons pine nuts

2 tablespoons raisins

½ teaspoon ground cinnamon

salt flakes and freshly cracked black pepper

Place the lard or butter and olive oil in the bowl of a stand mixer with the whisk attached and beat until combined. Add the orange juice and salt and mix on medium speed for a few minutes to form a paste.

Swap the whisk for the dough hook attachment, add the flour and knead for 4–5 minutes on medium speed until a dough forms. Wrap tightly in plastic wrap and refrigerate for 15–20 minutes.

Meanwhile, combine the vegetable filling ingredients in a bowl and set aside.

Preheat the oven to 170°C (340°F) fan-forced. Line two baking trays with baking paper.

Transfer the dough to a floured work surface and roll into a large log. Portion the dough into eighteen 75 g (2¾ oz) pieces and roll each one into a ball. Flatten the balls with the palms of your hands (grease your hands with a little oil if the dough is starting to stick) or use a rolling pin to roll the balls into 12 cm (4¾ in) circles.

Set aside on the prepared trays and place in the fridge for 10 minutes to firm up slightly.

Spoon 1 tablespoon of the filling in a thick line along the left side of one dough circle. Brush the edge with a little water and fold the empty side of the dough over the filling. Pinch the dough all the way around to form a seal. Repeat with the remaining dough and filling.

Bake for 40–45 minutes, until golden and cooked through.

Set the pasties aside on a wire rack to cool slightly and to allow the filling to continue cooking before serving.

Eat warm or at room temperature on a hot day.

Empanadas de cordero

Empanadas de verdura

Ricotta & quince turnovers

Many traditional dishes start in the family home, passed down through the generations. This is one of those recipes that unites everyone – made in a large batch by the whole family in a party atmosphere, and then shared among everyone at the end.

These turnovers are typically made with pumpkin jam and eaten at Christmas and Easter, but I love using ricotta and quince paste, especially at Christmas, to make a change from the regular cheese board.

Rubiols

100 g (3½ oz) lard or butter, at room temperature

2 tablespoons extra virgin olive oil

60 ml (¼ cup) freshly squeezed orange juice

2 tablespoons sweet white wine

1 egg yolk

100 g (3½ oz) caster (superfine) sugar

500 g (1 lb 2 oz) plain (all-purpose) flour, plus extra for dusting

Ricotta & quince filling

200 g (7 oz) good-quality firm ricotta

2 tablespoons caster (superfine) sugar

50 g (1¾ oz) quince paste, cut into small dice

Place the lard or butter and olive oil in the bowl of a stand mixer with the whisk attached and beat until combined. Add the orange juice, wine, egg yolk and sugar and mix on medium speed for a few minutes to form a paste.

Swap the whisk for the dough hook attachment, add the flour and knead for 4–5 minutes on medium speed until a dough forms. Cut the dough in half, wrap both halves tightly in plastic wrap and refrigerate for 15–20 minutes.

Meanwhile, to make the filling, combine the ricotta and sugar in a bowl and set aside.

Preheat the oven to 170°C (340°F) fan-forced. Line two baking trays with baking paper.

Working with one half of dough at a time, transfer the dough to a floured work surface and roll it out as thinly as possible.

Using a round 10 cm (4 in) cookie cutter, cut out as many circles as possible, re-rolling any dough offcuts, until it's all used up.

Place 1 tablespoon of the ricotta filling on one half of each dough circle, leaving a 1–1.5 cm (½ in) border and press a few cubes of quince paste into the filling.

Brush a little water around the edge, then fold over the unfilled half of dough and seal, using a fork to crimp the edges. Place on the prepared trays and bake for 20–25 minutes, until golden and cooked through (see Note).

Note

If you've used butter instead of lard, keep an eye on the turnovers as they cook as they'll colour more quickly.

Angel hair jam is a popular filling for pastries across Spain and its islands. It's made using the fibrous flesh of the siam pumpkin, which can be hard to get hold of, so here I've used spaghetti squash, which gives a similar stringy, thread-like result, only in a deep amber colour rather than the original transparent sweet jam that's enjoyed throughout the Iberian Peninsula.

Cabello de ángel y manzana

1 spaghetti squash, cut in half lengthways, seeds removed

3 red apples, peeled, roughly chopped

450 g (1 lb) caster (superfine) sugar

zest of ½ lemon

juice of 1 lemon

Preheat the oven to 200°C (400°F) fan-forced. Line a baking tray with baking paper.

Place the squash, flesh side down, on the prepared tray and bake for 30 minutes or until the skin starts to soften.

Allow to cool slightly, then scoop out the flesh into a saucepan – you should have about 1 kg (2 lb 3 oz). Add the apple, sugar, lemon zest and juice and gently cook over medium–low heat, stirring frequently, for 20–25 minutes, until the sugar has dissolved and the mixture has thickened.

If you are going to use the jam within a few days, set it aside in a bowl to cool, then keep covered in the fridge. Alternatively, transfer to two 500 ml (17 fl oz) sterilised jars (see Note opposite) while the jam is still hot, tightly seal and turn upside-down to cool. Once cool, put the jars through the dishwasher to clean and reinforce the seals.

The jam will keep in a cool, dry spot for 4–6 months.

Lemon marmalade

Marmalade was said to have been invented when a cargo of oranges washed up on the shores of Dundee, Scotland, after a Spanish ship ran aground during the British occupation of Menorca. You will find many British influences in the pastry shops on the island, from the humble sponge to meringues and lemon tart. Of course, lemons are a huge part of Mediterranean cuisine. We know they always accompany fish and they're even served in finger bowls to clean your hands, but marrying them with sugar to make marmalade? What a great way to enjoy their bitterness and acidity.

This lemon marmalade is a perfect spread or filling for any number of pastries you might indulge in. Serve it with freshly baked croissants or just simply with butter on toast.

Mermelada de limón

1 kg (2 lb 3 oz) lemons
800 g (1 lb 12 oz) caster (superfine) sugar
pinch of salt flakes
1 cinnamon stick
3 thyme sprigs

Clean the lemons, then place in a large saucepan, cover with water and bring to the boil. Reduce the heat to a simmer and cook for 45–60 minutes, until the lemons are soft when pierced with a knife. Drain and set aside to cool.

Slice the ends off the lemons and discard. Quarter the lemons and scoop out the flesh and seeds into a fine sieve set over a saucepan to act as a drip bowl underneath. Squash the flesh through the strainer into the saucepan, then place the remaining pulp and pips in a square of muslin (cheese cloth) and tie with kitchen string. Place in the saucepan with the lemon juice and flesh.

Remove any remaining white pith from the rind and cut the rind into even-sized strips as thick or as thin as you would like. Add the rind to the saucepan, along with the remaining ingredients and 250 ml (1 cup) of water. Bring to a rolling boil and stir until the sugar has dissolved, then reduce the heat to a simmer and cook for 20–30 minutes. The longer you cook the mixture, the stringier and darker the marmalade will be.

Remove and discard the cinnamon stick, then spoon the jam into a sterilised 600 ml (20½ fl oz) glass jar (see Note) while hot, then tightly seal and turn upside-down to cool. Once cool, put the jar through the dishwasher to clean and reinforce the heat seal.

The marmalade will keep in a cool, dry spot for 4–6 months.

Note
To sterilise glass jars, wash the jars and lids in hot, soapy water and remove any labels or residual food. Preheat the oven to 110°C (230°F) fan-forced, place the jars and lids upside down on clean wire racks and place in the oven for 10–12 minutes, until dry. Transfer to a clean tea towel, right side up, and fill as directed.

Cabello de ángel y manzana

Mermelada de limón

This dish is a very typical household soupy stew, using a little bit of this and that left over from the fishermen's catch in one big hotpot wonder.

It can get quite fancy in restaurants and on special occasions, with all kinds of shellfish, such as scampi and cockles or baby squid and scallops, or even lobster. This recipe is a simple, relatively inexpensive version, perfect for making at home.

Suquet de Pescado

2 tablespoons extra virgin olive oil

3 garlic cloves

3 ripe tomatoes, grated, skins discarded

2 teaspoons tomato paste (concentrated purée)

1 teaspoon salt flakes

400 g (14 oz) Dutch cream potatoes, peeled and sliced into 5 mm (¼ in) thick rounds

125 ml (½ cup) dry cooking sherry

about 400 ml (13½ fl oz) Caldo de pescado (see page 262) or store-bought fish stock

pinch of saffron threads

½ teaspoon sugar

1 tablespoon brandy

2 tablespoons Picada (see page 260)

4 x 180 g (6½ oz) trevally, king fish or hake cutlets

200 g (7 oz) firm white fish fillets, such as monkfish, blue eye, rock ling or flathead, cut into 4–5 cm (1½–2 in) chunks

8 large green prawns (shrimp), peeled and deveined, heads and tails left intact

8 mussels, scrubbed and debearded

crusty bread, to serve

Heat the olive oil in a flameproof casserole dish (Dutch oven) over medium heat. Add the garlic, tomato, tomato paste and salt and cook, stirring occasionally, for 10 minutes or until reduced and beginning to darken in colour. Add the potato, sherry, stock, saffron and sugar and give everything a good stir. Cover and simmer for 15 minutes, making sure the potato is fully submerged in the liquid – you may need to add a little more stock depending on the size of your saucepan.

Remove the lid, add the brandy and stir through the picada, then poke the fish pieces into the stew. Cook for 4–6 minutes, then add the prawns and mussels and cook for 2–3 minutes, until just cooked through and opened. Discard any mussels that do not open.

Serve the stew on the table in its dish with plenty of bread for mopping up all the delicious juices.

The *socarrat* that forms on the base of a paella while the rice is cooking is always the hero. It's this caramelised, crusty blanket that keeps you digging back for more.

Serving this dish with alioli is a must, it really makes this dramatic-looking paella come to life on the plate. Most connoisseurs of the arroz negro will mix alioli through their entire portion to coat it evenly, but I like to dip every mouthful into my garlicky mayonnaise blob and then drown it in plenty of freshly squeezed lemon.

Do seek out bomba or calasparra rice if you can. Supermarket medium-grain rice will suffice, but you'll notice the difference if you can track down the real thing.

Arroz negro

60 ml (¼ cup) extra virgin olive oil

2 garlic cloves, smashed open

2 red bullhorn peppers or 1 red capsicum (bell pepper), thinly sliced

1.2 litres (41 fl oz) Caldo de pescado (see page 262) or store-bought fish stock

pinch of saffron threads

3 x 8 g (¼ oz) sachets squid ink

420 g (1½ cups) Sofrito (see page 258)

250 g (9 oz) whole cuttlefish or calamari, cleaned and rinsed, hoods cut into diamonds or squares, tentacles set aside

150 g (5½ oz) small or medium peeled prawns (shrimp), roughly chopped

400 g (14 oz) short-grain rice, such as bomba or calasparra

80 ml (⅓ cup) dry sherry or white vermouth

300 g (10½ oz) clams (vongole) or pipis, soaked in cold water for 1 hour, drained

8 scampi

salt flakes

Alioli (see page 256), to serve

lemon wedges, to serve

Heat the olive oil in a 32–34 cm (12½–13¼ in) paella pan or frying pan over medium heat. Add the garlic and bullhorn pepper and cook, stirring occasionally, for 6–8 minutes, until the pepper is soft and its colour has run out into the oil. Transfer the pepper to a plate, leaving the garlic in the pan.

Meanwhile, heat the stock in a saucepan over medium heat and stir through the saffron and squid ink.

Add the sofrito and cuttlefish hoods to the paella pan and heat until sizzling. Cook, stirring frequently, for 5 minutes, then add the prawns and rice. Stir to coat the rice grains evenly, then pour in the sherry or vermouth and fold through until everything is really well combined.

Add half the stock to the pan and spread out the mixture, so it's in an even layer. Gently simmer over low heat for 6 minutes, shaking the pan back and forth every so often to loosen and aerate the rice.

When half the liquid has been absorbed, create a few little holes in the mixture using the end of a wooden spoon to help prevent the rice burning. You don't want to stir the mixture at this stage as this will disrupt the socarrat base and over-activate the starches in the rice. Rotate the pan around the burners on the stovetop if you see there isn't an even heat, so each side of the pan cooks evenly. Once the liquid has completely evaporated, place the clams or pipis and cuttlefish tentacles on top of the rice, then pour in the remaining stock. Cook for a further 6 minutes, giving the pan a little shake from time to time. When reduced by half again, add the scampi and red pepper and simmer for another 6 minutes, until the rice has absorbed all but a thin layer of liquid on top. Check the seasoning and add a little salt if necessary. The texture of the rice should be just al dente.

Remove from the heat, cover with newspaper (ink on ink!) or a clean (dark-coloured) tea towel and set aside for 6–8 minutes, to settle and absorb the remaining liquid.

Serve with alioli and lemon wedges.

Traditionally this dish was cooked in local beer made with farmers' hops and honey from the land, making it a much-loved classic. Today, thanks to the tourists' palate, a lot of good beers can be found in Spain and increasingly there are also a number of cool, local craft-beer companies making their way into bars, restaurants and hotels.

This dish normally uses a whole lamb shoulder chopped up by the local butcher, but I've used shanks here for ease and uniformity.

Cordero a la cervesa

4 x 375 g (13 oz) lamb shanks

salt flakes and freshly cracked black pepper

2 tablespoons light-flavoured extra virgin olive oil

150 g (5½ oz) pancetta, diced

2 celery stalks, finely diced

1 carrot, finely diced

3 garlic cloves, finely chopped

2 sprigs of rosemary, leaves picked

8 spring onions (scallions), white part only, roughly chopped

330 ml (11 fl oz) bottle strong lager or beer

1 litre (4 cups) chicken or vegetable stock

Score three or four slits in the flesh of each shank and season with salt and pepper.

Preheat the oven to 180°C (350°F) fan-forced.

Heat half the olive oil in a flameproof casserole dish over high heat, add the lamb shanks and sear on all sides, until golden. Transfer the lamb to a plate and set aside.

Wipe out the pan to remove any remaining stuck-on bits and reduce the heat to medium–high. Add the remaining oil and the pancetta and cook for 4–5 minutes, until beginning to crisp, then add the celery and carrot and cook for 12–15 minutes, until soft. Add the garlic, rosemary and spring onion, stir for 2 minutes, then add the beer and simmer until the liquid reduces to a syrup.

Pour in the stock, bring to the boil, then reduce the heat to medium and simmer for 5 minutes. Return the lamb to the pan, cover and place in the oven for 30 minutes.

Reduce the temperature to 160°C (320°F) and bake for a further 1½ hours. Increase the temperature back up to 180°C (350°F), remove the lid and cook for a final 30 minutes or until the tops of the shanks colour slightly and the sauce has reduced a little.

Serve the lamb shanks with your favourite purée, such as celeriac, parsnip, cauliflower or good old-fashioned mashed potato and loads of sauce, and wash it all down with a nice cold beer.

A Sunday-night takeaway summer classic for when it's too hot to turn on the oven or too much effort to cook after a weekend at the beach. Every town has a local chicken shop that sells rotisserie chicken, which locals pick on up their way home and serve simply with *patatas*.

This all-seasons recipe can be made in the afternoon and left to slowly cook on the barbecue while you have a siesta, potter in the garden or simply relax with a good book.

Pollo a la brasa

1 x 1.6 kg (3½ lb) free-range chicken, rinsed

60 ml (¼ cup) extra virgin olive oil

4 large potatoes, halved

2 teaspoons fine sea salt

1 teaspoon onion powder

½ teaspoon garlic powder

½ teaspoon smoked pimentón

1 teaspoon dried oregano

½ teaspoon ground white pepper

125 ml (½ cup) dry white wine

salt flakes

Salsa verde (see page 259), to serve

Alioli (see page 256), to serve

Dislocate the chicken hips by placing it breast side down and using your thumbs to push the tops of the thigh joints in on themselves towards the breast and then out away from the chicken frame. Pat the chicken dry inside and out with paper towel, then place in the fridge to air-dry for 2 hours.

Preheat a barbecue or smoker to high (220°C/440°F).

Drizzle 2 tablespoons of the olive oil over the potato halves, sprinkle with half the salt and wrap each potato half in foil.

Remove the chicken from the fridge and rub with the remaining olive oil.

Combine the onion and garlic powders, pimentón, oregano, white pepper and remaining salt in a small bowl, then evenly dust all over the chicken.

Place the chicken, breast side up, on a wire rack and sit in a large baking dish. Pour the wine and 500 ml (2 cups) of water into the dish, then transfer to the barbecue, close the lid and cook for 20 minutes, before reducing the heat to low (120°C/240°F). Open the lid, throw the potatoes on the grill plate and turn the chicken over. Close the lid and leave to cook for 1½ hours. Turn the chicken over one more time, pour another 500 ml (2 cups) water into the base of the dish and cook for a further 1 hour.

Turn the heat off and let the chicken rest inside the barbecue for 20 minutes before carving.

Crack open the baked potatoes, sprinkle with salt flakes and serve with your favourite cut of chicken, plenty of salsa verde and mountains of alioli.

Bullit de pescado is the epitome of Ibizan gastronomy, and it's likely to be the first dish a local recommends you to try. Translated as 'boiled fish', it's served in two parts, so you want to make a day of it, which is usually Sunday for the locals. First up, great-quality fish is poached (with or without potatoes, contentiously) and then served with a rich alioli. The stock is then used to cook Arroz a banda (see opposite) for the second course. This crunchy-bottomed, exquisitely simple rice is one of the best things I've ever eaten.

If you like, you can add potato and forget about the rice, or do as the locals do and feast your Sunday away in gluttony.

Bullit de pescado

2 x 300 g (10½ oz) whole fish, such as rock fish, red emperor, monkfish, rock ling, red snapper or leather jacket, cleaned and gutted

4 x 160 g (5½ oz) fish cutlets, such as trevally, hake or king fish

100 g (3½ oz) fine sea salt

freshly cracked black pepper

2 tablespoons extra virgin olive oil

1 onion, finely diced

2 garlic cloves, minced

salt flakes

2 tomatoes, grated, skins discarded

1 green capsicum (bell pepper), cut into 8 chunks

250 ml (1 cup) dry white wine

2 pinches of saffron threads

3 litres (3 qts) Caldo de pescado (see page 262) or store-bought fish stock, heated to a simmer

4 potatoes, peeled and halved

4 raw scampi

300 g (10½ oz) Roman or flat (runner) beans, trimmed and halved

1 x quantity Alioli (see page 256), plus extra to serve

2 lemons, halved

Remove the heads from the whole fish and cut the fish in half crossways.

Salt the fish cutlets and fish with the sea salt and some black pepper and set aside in a large colander in the sink for 30 minutes.

Heat the olive oil in a large saucepan over medium heat. Add the onion, garlic and a pinch of salt flakes and cook for 15 minutes or until soft and cooked down to a paste. Add the tomato and cook for 6–8 minutes, until incorporated and broken down, then add the capsicum and stir for 1 minute. Pour in the white wine and add the saffron, fish stock and potato, then bring to a simmer and cook for 8–10 minutes, until slightly reduced. One by one, add the fish and scampi, then reduce the heat to low and simmer for 5 minutes. Add the beans and cook for a further 4–5 minutes, until the fish is firm and the potato is cooked through. Using a large slotted spoon, gently transfer the fish, scampi, potato, beans and capsicum to a large serving platter. Cover with foil and keep warm while you finish the sauce.

Strain 500 ml (2 cups) of the fish stock into a large jug and strain the remaining stock into a container to use for the second course, Arroz a banda.

Once the stock in the jug has cooled a little, add 2 tablespoons to the alioli and whisk to combine. Continue to add the liquid in this way until you reach a cream consistency.

Spoon the sauce over the fish and vegetables and serve with extra alioli and the lemon halves.

Originating from Alicante, *a banda*, meaning 'apart', is a fisherman's paella simply made using the leftovers from the daily catch, boiled up into a stock, along with a few pieces of fish reserved for the top of the paella.

Over on Formentera and Ibiza, this traditional favourite is usually served with the fish on the side (hence its name) in the form of the fish stew Bullit de pescado (see opposite). I also like to serve it this way, but this rice dish is equally satisfying on its own with a chunky garden salad. Always, always serve with more alioli than you think you'll need, and if you're considering serving both dishes, make a double batch and reserve half of it for the bullit sauce.

Arroz a banda

2 tablespoons extra virgin olive oil

1 onion, finely chopped

2 garlic cloves, finely chopped

salt flakes

150 g (5½ oz) calamari hoods, cleaned and finely minced

200 g (7 oz) small peeled raw prawns (shrimp)

2 large tomatoes, grated, skins discarded

2 teaspoons sweet pimentón

250 ml (1 cup) white wine

200 g (7 oz) short-grain rice, such as bomba or calasparra

freshly cracked black pepper

1 litre (4 cups) Caldo de pescado (see page 262) or store-bought fish stock, heated to a simmer, plus extra if needed

pinch of saffron threads

lemon wedges, to serve

Alioli (see page 256), to serve

Heat the olive oil in a large 32–34 cm (12¾–13½ in) paella pan or frying pan over medium heat. Add the onion, garlic and a pinch of salt flakes and sauté for 12–15 minutes, until soft. Stir through the calamari and cook for 3–4 minutes, until starting to turn golden. Add the prawns and stir through, then add the grated tomato and pimentón and cook for a further 5 minutes or until you have a deep-coloured, thick paste. Pour in the wine and cook until completely evaporated, then add the rice and stir well to coat the grains. Season with black pepper.

Add three-quarters of the stock and the saffron, and keep stirring until the mixture comes to the boil. Reduce the heat to medium–low and gently simmer for 12–15 minutes, until most of the liquid has evaporated. If you're unable to achieve an even heat, rotate the pan around the burners on the stovetop, so that each side of the pan cooks evenly. Pour in the remaining stock, then gently shake the pan from side to side to distribute the liquid. If you don't trust the surface of your pan, create a few holes in the mixture using the end of a wooden spoon or spatula to check if the base is burning. If so, reduce the heat to the lowest possible setting and add a little more stock if the pan is very dry. Continue to simmer over low heat for a further 6–8 minutes, until the rice is cooked through.

Remove from the heat and serve immediately in bowls with lemon wedges and alioli on the side and the fish stew opposite, if you're game.

Bullit de pescado

Arroz a banda

Dirty rice

There's nothing unclean about this dish! The title refers to the rustic, seasonal and intensely flavoured nature of this Spanish winter rice. The island cousin of the paella, dirty rice shares its family roots with a good *sofrito*, as all good Spanish rice dishes do. It's made with whatever is seasonally on hand, so you might find thrushes, quail or partridge (giblets and all) included, along with snails, vegetable-patch pickings or wild mushrooms, all of which contribute to that 'dirty', earthy flavour.

Arroz del campo

2 tablespoons extra virgin
   olive oil

1 pork spare rib, cut into 1.5 cm
   (½ in) dice

200 g (7 oz) chicken ribs

200 g (7 oz) rabbit (or use a
   boneless chicken thigh fillet),
   cut into 2–3 cm (¾–1¼ in)
   chunks

4 artichoke hearts in brine,
   halved

1 red capsicum (bell pepper),
   thinly sliced

1 onion, chopped

3 garlic cloves, chopped

2 teaspoons sweet pimentón

125 ml (½ cup) dry white wine

2 large tomatoes, grated, skins
   discarded

400 g (14 oz) short-grain rice,
   such as bomba or calasparra

1.5 litres (6 cups) chicken stock,
   heated to a simmer

pinch of saffron threads

8–12 prepared snails (optional)

8 asparagus spears, cut into
   2 cm (¾ in) lengths

150 g (5½ oz) runner (flat)
   beans, trimmed, cut into 2 cm
   (¾ in) lengths

100 g (⅔ cup) frozen peas

lemon wedges, to serve

Heat half the olive oil in a large 32–34 cm (12¾–13½ in) paella pan or frying pan over medium heat. Working in batches, cook the pork, chicken, rabbit and artichoke until seared and golden brown on all sides. Remove from the pan and set aside on a large plate.

Wipe out the pan to remove any stuck-on bits, then add the remaining oil along with the capsicum and gently sauté over medium–low heat for 8–10 minutes, until soft and the colour has leached out of the capsicum into the oil. Remove the capsicum from the pan and set aside on a small plate.

Add the onion and garlic to the pan and cook over medium–low heat for 12–15 minutes, until soft and beginning to disintegrate. Stir through the pimentón and cook for 3–4 minutes, then pour in the white wine and cook for 6–8 minutes, until completely evaporated. Add the grated tomato and cook for a further 15 minutes or until the mixture becomes a rich-coloured thick paste. Add the rice and stir to coat the grains. Stir through the reserved meats, artichoke and capsicum, along with three-quarters of the stock and the saffron.

Bring the mixture to the boil, then reduce the heat to low and simmer for 10 minutes. If you're unable to achieve an even heat, rotate the pan around the burners on the stovetop so that each side of the pan cooks evenly. Pour in the remaining stock, add the snails (if using), asparagus and beans and gently shake the pan from side to side. Check the bottom with a spoon if you fear it may be catching and reduce the heat, if possible. Continue to simmer for 8–10 minutes, until the rice is cooked through. Scatter over the peas and cook for a final 2 minutes.

Remove from the heat and serve immediately with lemon wedges on the side.

Spanish families will serve this dish at least once over the Christmas festive period and it's particularly popular at New Year's Eve (Nochebuena) celebrations. It's also not complete without potatoes! Sometimes a *picada* will be spooned over the top – if you'd like to try this, add a pinch of saffron to the recipe on page 260 and spoon it over the lamb shoulder just before serving, instead of the herbs.

Paletilla de cordero al horno

500 g (1 lb 2 oz) rock salt

2 sprigs of rosemary

2 fresh bay leaves

1 cinnamon stick, halved

8 juniper berries

2–2.5 kg (4 lb 6 oz–5½ lb) lamb shoulder, bone in

1 tablespoon extra virgin olive oil

1 teaspoon freshly cracked black pepper

125 ml (½ cup) sherry vinegar

125 ml (½ cup) dry white wine

2 garlic bulbs, cut in half crossways

2 lemons, halved

500 g (1 lb 2 oz) chat (baby) potatoes

1 teaspoon salt flakes

mixed fresh herbs, such as mint, dill, parsley, basil and tarragon leaves, to serve

In a blender, blitz the salt, one rosemary sprig, one bay leaf, half the cinnamon and the juniper berries until evenly chopped.

Place the lamb in a large baking dish and rub with the salt mix to coat. Set aside in the fridge for 2 hours.

Preheat the oven to 230°C (445°F) fan-forced.

Rub the salt off the lamb and rinse well. Pat dry with paper towel and allow to air-dry on a wire rack at room temperature for 30 minutes.

Smear the lamb with the olive oil and sprinkle with the pepper. Place the lamb and the wire rack on top of a baking dish and pour the vinegar, wine and 1 litre (4 cups) of water into the base of the dish. Throw in the garlic, two lemon halves and the remaining rosemary, bay leaf and cinnamon. Roast for 30 minutes, then remove from the oven and turn the shoulder over. Reduce the temperature to 150°C (300°F) and return the lamb to the oven and roast for a further 30 minutes. Remove, turn the lamb again and place the potatoes in the baking dish. Return to the oven for another 30 minutes. Keep an eye on the liquid and add a little more water if the baking dish is dry and the potatoes are starting to burn. Finally, increase the heat back to 230°C (445°F), turn the lamb shoulder one last time and roast for 15 minutes.

Transfer the lamb and potatoes to a serving dish. Squeeze the remaining lemon halves over the potatoes and sprinkle with the salt. Scatter the herbs over the lamb and serve.

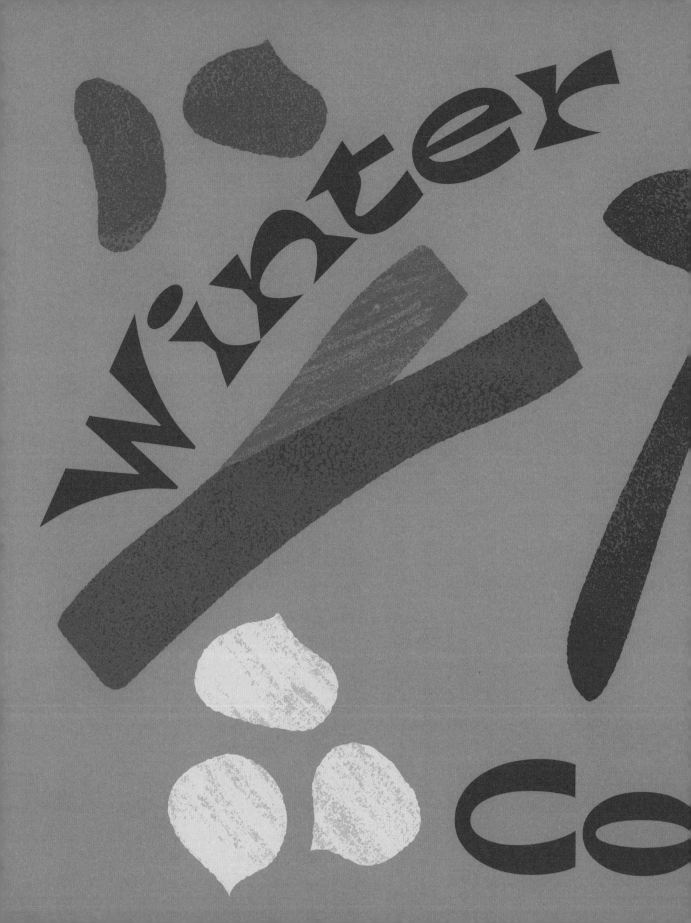

Most of Spain enjoys a year-round Mediterranean climate, with mild winter months, especially in the east and south of the country. Throughout the cooler seasons, summer produce is replaced with more hearty fare. The aromas of stews, broths and soups fill Spanish kitchens as well as slow-cooked braises of pork and lamb.

Each province will adapt these traditional dishes, swapping in ingredients based on what's locally availble. Foraging is still a popular activity, rewarding the dedicated and patient with varieties of mushrooms, winter leafy greens and herbs that can be added to the pot.

In some rural areas of Spain, the *matanza* – a traditional pig slaughter – is an important community event that still happens between November and February every year. Starting in the early hours of the morning, family and friends gather for a long day of work and festivities, where every part of the animal is butchered, classified and turned into quality charcuterie and prime cuts for the year ahead. Thankfully, you don't have to slaughter your own pig to enjoy the pork dishes in this chapter.

Dried beans and legumes are other popular ingredients; historically added to meat stews and soups for bulk and sustenance when times were lean, today Spanish dried beans are revered throughout Europe. The pork loin medallions in milk with white beans in this chapter is a typical example of the Spanish marriage between beans and pork. Traditionally a farmhouse stew, it is actually a rather sophisticated dish that makes the perfect winter dinner-party centrepiece.

Chestnuts are one of Spain's most popular street foods – their sweet, nutty aroma fills town plazas around the country, crackling and blistering over wood-fired gallon drums. Here, they are paired with earthy mushrooms, resulting in a poetic union of warmth and comfort to help see in the cooler months.

Crema de castañas con setas

1 kg (2 lb 3 oz) chestnuts

120 g (4½ oz) butter

2 tablespoons extra virgin olive oil

1 leek, white part only, thinly sliced

salt flakes and freshly cracked black pepper

1 turnip, swede (rutabaga) or parsnip (about 250 g/9 oz), peeled and diced

2 litres (2 qts) vegetable stock, heated

100 ml (3½ fl oz) pouring (single/light) cream

200 g (7 oz) assorted mushrooms, such as pine, saffron caps, chestnut, king brown, Swiss brown and button, thickly sliced

2 garlic cloves, thinly sliced (or young garlic shoots if you can find them)

2 sprigs of thyme

60 ml (¼ cup) dry cooking sherry

Preheat the oven to 180°C (350°F) fan-forced.

Using a small serrated knife, score the top of each chestnut with a cross. Transfer to a wire rack set over a roasting tin and roast for 20 minutes, or until they begin to split open.

Transfer the chestnuts to a large heatproof bowl and cover tightly with plastic wrap to steam for 10 minutes. Peel the nuts and set aside, discarding the shells.

Heat half the butter and 1 tablespoon of the olive oil in a large heavy-based saucepan over medium heat. Add the leek and a pinch of salt and cook, stirring occasionally, for 4–6 minutes, until soft. Add the peeled chestnuts, your root vegetable of choice and stir to coat, then pour in the vegetable stock. Increase the heat to high and bring to a high simmer for 20 minutes, until the liquid has reduced by one-third. Reduce the heat to low, then carefully purée the soup using a hand-held blender. Simmer the soup for a little longer if you prefer a thicker result.

Remove from the heat and strain through a fine sieve to remove any raw chestnut pieces. Whisk through the cream and season to taste.

Heat the remaining olive oil and 1 teaspoon of the remaining butter in a frying pan over medium–high heat. Add the mushrooms and cook, stirring, until sizzling. Add the garlic and thyme and cook for 4–6 minutes, until the mushrooms are soft and any liquid has reduced. Add the sherry and reduce by half, then remove from the heat and immediately stir through the remaining butter.

Divide the soup among bowls and top with the sautéed mushrooms.

This flexible soup is a much-loved family favourite on the island of Mallorca. The vegetables change with the seasons, but the bread – usually a light rye or farmhouse loaf – is non-negotiable and transforms this simple dish from a light lunch into a hearty meal. It's a great way to use up day-old bread, as it soaks up the broth and gives the soup bulk and texture.

Sopa Mallorquina

½ loaf light rye bread

2 tomatoes

iced water

1½ tablespoons extra virgin olive oil, plus extra for drizzling

150 g (5½ oz) piece of pork spare ribs, roughly chopped into 1 cm (½ in) pieces

1 tablespoon sobrassada (see page 8)

1 leek, white part only, finely chopped

3 garlic cloves, finely chopped

¼ head of cauliflower, cut into small florets

200 g (7 oz) shredded savoy cabbage

4 sprigs of marjoram or oregano

2 teaspoons sweet pimentón

1 litre (4 cups) vegetable or chicken stock

100 g (3½ oz) green beans, trimmed, cut into 2.5 cm (1 in) lengths

150 g (5½ oz) baby English spinach leaves

salt flakes and freshly cracked black pepper

½ bunch chives, finely snipped

Preheat the oven to 170°C (340°F) fan-forced.

Place the bread in the freezer for 30–60 minutes, to harden a little before slicing. Using a sharp bread knife, slice the bread as thinly as possible, then transfer to a baking tray in a single layer and bake for 6 minutes to dry out.

Using a sharp knife, score a cross in the base of the tomatoes. Bring a saucepan of water to the boil and blanch the tomatoes for 2 minutes or until the skins start to curl away from the flesh. Immediately drain and plunge into iced water, then peel away the skins and cut the flesh into quarters. Remove and discard the seeds and roughly chop the flesh.

Heat the olive oil in a large saucepan over medium–high heat. Add the pork ribs and cook for 4–5 minutes, until golden brown, then add the sobrassada, leek and garlic and cook, stirring, for 3–4 minutes, until the leek softens slightly. Add the chopped tomato and cook, stirring, for 2 minutes, then reduce the heat to medium–low and add the cauliflower, cabbage, marjoram or oregano and pimentón. Cook for 8–10 minutes, until the vegetables are soft but not caramelised. Pour in the stock, cover with a lid and increase the heat to high. Remove the lid as soon as the mixture starts to boil and add the beans. Simmer for 4–6 minutes, until the beans are cooked through, then remove from the heat, stir through the spinach and season to taste with salt and pepper.

Ladle the soup into bowls and gently place the bread slices on top. Drizzle with a little oil and serve, garnished with the chives.

The name of this recipe translates to poor man's potatoes, but don't be fooled by the name! It's a rich and elegant side dish, and a Spanish favourite to accompany grilled meat, poultry or fish. Try to track down locally grown good-quality potatoes if you can, as they will make a huge difference to the flavour of the finished dish.

Patatas a lo pobre

125 ml (½ cup) extra virgin olive oil

1 kg (2 lb 3 oz) Dutch cream potatoes, peeled and sliced about 3 mm (⅛ in) thick

1 onion, sliced into rounds

3 garlic cloves, slit down one side

1 green capsicum (bell pepper), sliced

170 ml (⅔ cup) vegetable or chicken stock, heated

salt flakes and freshly cracked black pepper

Heat the olive oil in a wide heavy-based saucepan over medium–high heat. Add all the ingredients to the pan and give everything a stir.

Reduce the heat to medium–low, cover and cook for 6–8 minutes. Remove the lid and continue to cook until the oil has been absorbed and the potato is cooked through (add a little extra water if necessary to prevent the potato burning and sticking to the base of the pan).

Season to taste and serve straight away with your choice of meat, fish or poultry.

The chickpea is arguably Spain's most cherished legume, having arrived with Phoenician settlers nearly 3000 years ago where it flourished in the country's temperate climate. Such is the popularity of this humble ingredient, fresh chickpeas are often sold in large refrigerated tubs throughout the region of Catalonia, where they are added to stews, soups, salads and braises, such as this simple, nutritious and inexpensive dish that has long been cherished all over the Iberian Peninsula. This recipe uses dried chickpeas, but if you're short on time you can also use good-quality tinned chickpeas in a pinch.

Acelgas con garbanzos

200 g (7 oz) dried chickpeas (garbanzo beans), soaked in cold water overnight or 1 x 400 g (14 oz) tin chickpeas, rinsed and drained

3 garlic cloves, 2 slit down one side, 1 finely chopped

2 fresh bay leaves

2 tablespoons extra virgin olive oil

1 onion, finely diced

1 teaspoon fennel seeds

½ cinnamon stick

1 teaspoon ground allspice

bunch of silverbeet (Swiss chard), stems separated from leaves, both roughly chopped

185 ml (¾ cup) vegetable stock

2 lemons

salt flakes and freshly cracked black pepper

If using dried chickpeas, drain them and place in a large saucepan. Cover with plenty of water, the slit garlic cloves and the bay leaves. Bring to the boil over medium–high heat and cook for 50–70 minutes (larger and older chickpeas will take longer to cook). Drain and discard the garlic and bay leaves. Skip this step if using tinned chickpeas.

Heat the olive oil in a large frying pan over medium–high heat. Add the onion and cook for 6 minutes, or until beginning to soften. Add the finely chopped garlic, fennel seeds, cinnamon and allspice and stir well to combine.

Add the sliverbeet stems and vegetable stock to the pan and cook for 4–5 minutes, then add the chickpeas and the juice of 1 lemon. Continue to cook, until the chickpeas are heated through, then season to taste and mix in the silverbeet leaves until just wilted.

Transfer to shallow bowls, squeeze over the remaining lemon and sprinkle with some extra cracked pepper.

Braised broad beans with fideos

Throughout Spain, you will find many varieties of this beloved heavy winter stew. This Balearic *potaje*, with black pudding, pasta and dried broad (fava) beans, can be as sophisticated or simple as you like, and here I've used unpeeled dried broad beans, which makes a much chunkier version than the original, but I love how they allow me to chew my way through this substantial meal. If you prefer, you can also blitz the cooked beans with a good stock before adding the pasta.

Potaje de habas

2 tablespoons extra virgin olive oil, plus extra for drizzling

1 leek, white part only, finely chopped

3 garlic cloves, crushed

50 g (1¾ oz) sobrassada (see page 8), de-cased fresh chorizo or 1 teaspoon sweet pimentón

50 g (1¾ oz) black pudding, de-cased

3 tomatoes, halved and grated, skins discarded

2 litres (2 qts) vegetable or chicken stock

1 small pig's trotter, halved (ask your butcher to do this for you) or 1 pig's ear

300 g (10½ oz) dried broad (fava) beans, soaked in cold water overnight, drained

250 g (9 oz) pork spare ribs

150 g (5½ oz) thick fideos or spaghetti no. 5, cut into 4 cm (1½ in) lengths

1 teaspoon marjoram or oregano leaves

salt flakes and freshly cracked black pepper

crusty bread, to serve

Heat the olive oil, leek and garlic in a large heavy-based saucepan over medium–low heat. Cook, stirring occasionally, for 6–8 minutes, until the leek begins to soften. Stir through the sobrassada, chorizo or pimentón and black pudding and cook for 3 minutes. Add the tomato and cook for 6–8 minutes, until the tomato has reduced and darkened in colour.

Increase the heat to medium, then pour in the stock and add the pig's trotter or ear and broad beans. Bring to a simmer and cook, semi-covered, for 50–60 minutes, until reduced. Add the pork spare ribs and poach for 15 minutes or until cooked through. Remove the spare ribs from the pan and cut into even chunks. Return the ribs to the pan, add the fideos and marjoram or oregano and simmer for 10–12 minutes, until the pasta is cooked through.

Season to taste with salt and plenty of pepper and serve it up with some crusty bread and a drizzle of oil.

You will always find this dish on local *menu del dia* blackboards at lunchtime, served with hand-cut chips and an umami-filled mushroom sauce. Locally foraged mushrooms are the traditional choice for this fricassee, so choose your own adventure and include whatever shapes, textures and aromas are available to you – I make it differently every time. I also add a little teaspoon of red miso that brings the dish closer to those rich umami and salty flavours.

Fricandó de ternera

4 dried porcini mushrooms

110 g (¾ cup) plain (all-purpose) flour

sea salt and freshly cracked black pepper

800 g (1 lb 12 oz) skirt or flank steak (or veal rump steak), cut into 1 cm (½ in) thick slices

60 ml (¼ cup) extra virgin olive oil

1 onion, sliced

3 garlic cloves, crushed

2 sprigs of thyme

250 ml (1 cup) dry white wine

3 tomatoes, halved and grated, skins discarded

2 teaspoons dried oregano

1 teaspoon red miso paste

600 ml (20½ fl oz) Fondo oscuro de ternera (see page 263) or store-bought beef or veal stock

150 g (5½ oz) portobello mushrooms, sliced

150 g (5½ oz) small button mushrooms

150 g (5½ oz) oyster or shiitake mushrooms

1 x quantity Picada (see page 260)

1 litre (4 cups) vegetable oil

4 large potatoes, cut into 2 cm (¾ in) thick chips

Rehydrate the porcini mushrooms in a small bowl of boiling water for 15 minutes. Drain and set aside.

Flour and season the steak and dust off any excess.

Heat half the olive oil in a large frying pan over medium–high heat and, working in batches, sear the steak on both sides, until a thin golden crust forms. Transfer to a plate and set aside.

Add the remaining oil and the onion to the pan and cook, stirring frequently, for 6–8 minutes, until the onion starts to soften. Add the garlic, one thyme sprig and a pinch of salt and continue to cook until the onion starts to turn golden, then add the wine, grated tomato and oregano. Cook for 10–15 minutes, until most of the liquid has evaporated and the tomato starts to darken a little, then stir through the miso and add the meat back to the pan, along with the stock. Bring to a simmer, then reduce the heat to medium–low and add all the mushrooms. Simmer for 8–10 minutes, until the sauce has reduced and thickened and the meat is tender. Stir through the picada.

Meanwhile, heat the vegetable oil in a large frying pan over medium heat and shallow-fry the chips, turning frequently, for 15–18 minutes, until golden brown and cooked through. Drain on paper towel and sprinkle with salt.

Divide the steak and mushroom sauce among plates and serve with the chips to dip into all that mushroom goodness.

Shepherd's stew

This shepherd's stew encapsulates the flavours synonymous with Spain's mountainous region, where free-range sheep graze on wild native herbs, such as thyme, rosemary and marjoram. I like to add a little ground coriander and fennel seed as well to this dish to add even more of the floral, mountainous notes that pair so wonderfully with the strong taste of the local hillside lamb.

Caldereta de cordero

60 ml (¼ cup) extra virgin olive oil

3 garlic cloves, unpeeled, smashed

1 kg (2 lb 3 oz) lamb neck chops, cut in half, leaving the bones attached to one half

salt flakes and freshly cracked black pepper

1½ onions, finely diced

1 large carrot, finely diced

1 fresh bay leaf

2 sprigs of thyme

3 sprigs of oregano or marjoram

1 sprig of rosemary

1 teaspoon sweet pimentón

1 teaspoon ground coriander

1 teaspoon ground fennel seeds

½ teaspoon ground white pepper

3 tomatoes, halved

1 tablespoon tomato paste (concentrated purée)

60 ml (¼ cup) brandy or cognac

1 litre (4 cups) Fondo oscuro de ternera (see page 263) or use store-bought beef or veal stock

1 x 400 g (14 oz) tin white beans, such as cannellini, haricot (navy) or great northern, rinsed and drained

crusty baguette, to serve

Heat a large heavy-based stockpot with half the olive oil and the garlic over medium–high heat. Season the lamb with salt and pepper, add to the pan and sear on both sides until golden. Reduce the heat to medium–low, add the remaining oil, the onion, carrot, herbs, spices and 1 teaspoon of salt and sauté for 10 minutes, until the vegetables are soft and starting to colour.

Grate the tomatoes using a coarse grater and discard the skin. Add the tomato and tomato paste to the pot, stir well and cook for 2 minutes, then add the brandy and stock. Cook, with the lid ajar, for 40 minutes, then add the beans. Increase the heat to high and cook at a rapid simmer, uncovered, for a further 20 minutes to reduce the liquid.

Serve with a crusty baguette on the side.

This dish requires a gentle hand, as you don't want the milk to curdle. The almonds help to prevent this, but you will inevitably notice some of the impurities rising to the top. My instincts are always to 'skim the scum', but think of this as an off-white, or ivory, still-life Renaissance dish and resist the temptation. Thankfully, blending it at the end brings everything happily back together in this classic farmhouse stew.

Cerdo a la leche con alubias blancas

800 g–1 kg (1 lb 12 oz–2 lb 3 oz) pork loin medallion, cut into 8 steaks

salt flakes and ground white pepper

80 ml (⅓ cup) extra virgin olive oil

2 garlic cloves, halved

1 fresh bay leaf

10 black or white peppercorns

¼ nutmeg, freshly grated

40 g (¼ cup) blanched almonds

1 litre (4 cups) full-cream (whole) milk

250 g (9 oz) dried white beans, such as mongetes or ganxet, soaked in cold water overnight (or 1 x 400 g/14 oz tin white beans, rinsed and drained)

1 sprig of rosemary plus 1 teaspoon finely chopped rosemary leaves

salt flakes and freshly cracked black pepper

2 red or white witlof (Belgian endive/chicory), halved lengthways

½ teaspoon pink peppercorns

Season the pork steaks with sea salt and white pepper. Heat half the olive oil in a large frying pan or heavy-based saucepan over high heat. Working in batches, add the steaks and sear for 2–3 minutes each side, then transfer to a plate and strain off any excess oil in the pan.

Reduce the heat to medium–high and add the garlic, bay leaf, whole peppercorns, nutmeg and almonds to the pan. Stir and cook until the almonds start to toast and the garlic begins to brown. Pour in the milk and bring to a gentle simmer for 20 minutes. Remove from the heat, discard the bay leaf and blitz the sauce using a hand-held blender until smooth. Add the steaks to the blended milk and simmer over low heat for a further 20 minutes.

Meanwhile, drain the beans and place in a large saucepan with the rosemary sprig. Cover with cold water and bring to the boil. Reduce the heat and simmer for 35–40 minutes, until tender, then drain and place the beans in a bowl. Remove and discard the rosemary sprig and add 1 tablespoon of the remaining olive oil, the chopped rosemary and plenty of salt and pepper. Combine well. If using tinned beans, rinse and drain and combine in a bowl with the oil, chopped rosemary and seasoning.

Coat the witlof in the remaining olive oil and chargrill or pan-fry over high heat for 2 minutes each side to slightly colour.

Serve the pork loins in their sauce with the white beans and grilled witlof on the side, and with the pink peppercorns sprinkled over the top.

This is an inexpensive cut of the pig to try, but you want to get the cheek with the jowl still attached as this is where all the flavour is. This is a deep, hearty, rich, sticky and gelatinous dish that's best cooked as a braise. It's also great to put in a slow cooker in the morning and forget about for the rest of the day.

As autumn turns into winter, it's very traditional to find this dish on local restaurant menus to coincide with the season for butchering and making sausages. The orange flavour of the fresh 'picada' goes fantastically with the pork – just like an Italian gremolata served with osso bucco.

Carrilleras de cerdo

80 ml (⅓ cup) extra virgin olive oil

4 x 300 g (10½ oz) pork cheeks, jowls attached

1 garlic bulb, halved crossways

1 large leek, white part only, finely chopped

120 g (4½ oz) smoky bacon rashers (slices), finely diced

4 sprigs of thyme

2 tablespoons tomato paste (concentrated purée)

4–6 vine-ripened tomatoes, larger ones halved

750 ml (3 cups) dry red wine

6–8 parsnips, larger ones halved

½ teaspoon ground cinnamon

salt flakes and freshly cracked black pepper

1 orange, zested and halved

6–8 cipollini, shallots or small pickling onions, peeled

1 litre (4 cups) Fondo oscuro de ternera (see page 263) or store-bought beef stock

40 g (¼ cup) blanched almonds, toasted, finely chopped

handful of chopped parsley leaves

crusty bread, to serve

Preheat the oven to 180°C (350°F) fan-forced.

Heat 2 tablespoons of the olive oil in a large flameproof casserole dish over high heat and sear the pork cheeks for 6 minutes each side until golden. Remove the cheeks from the dish and set aside.

Add the garlic, leek, bacon and thyme to the dish, reduce the heat to medium and cook for 12–15 minutes, until softened and starting to colour. Add the tomato paste and tomatoes and cook for 4 minutes, stirring constantly to avoid burning. Add half the wine and simmer for 30 minutes, or until reduced by half.

Meanwhile, line a roasting tin with baking paper. Place the parsnips in the tin and toss with 1 tablespoon of the remaining oil, the cinnamon and some salt and pepper.

Return the cheeks to the dish and add the remaining wine, then squeeze over the orange halves and add the cipollini and stock. Season with salt and pepper, then transfer to the middle rack of the oven and roast for 30 minutes.

Pop the parsnips in the oven and turn the cheeks over if they're not completely submerged in the liquid. Roast for a further 30 minutes.

Make a fresh 'picada' by combining the almonds, parsley, orange zest and remaining oil in a small bowl. Season with salt and pepper, to taste.

Divide the cheeks among plates and serve with plenty of the sauce. Sprinkle the picada over the top and serve with the roasted parsnips and crusty bread on the side.

A festive specialty of the Pityuses, which includes the islands of Ibiza and Formentera, this farmer's pot was once considered too expensive to eat regularly. Unlike fish, which locals caught for themselves and maybe a neighbour, or an inexpensive island chicken, pork and lamb were considered a luxury. The meat, seasonal vegetables and local herbs and spices from the garden were traditionally cooked only at Christmas time, but today you'll find it on menus and in locals' kitchens year-round.

Sofrito Payés

1 kg (2 lb 3 oz) bone-in lamb neck or shoulder, cut into 8 pieces (ask your butcher to do this for you)

4 fresh bay leaves

2 skinless chicken thigh cutlets, cut in half

250 ml (1 cup) extra virgin olive oil

2 good-quality pork sausages, cut into 8 pieces

2 fresh chorizo sausages, cut into 8 pieces

½ green capsicum (bell pepper)

½ red capsicum (bell pepper)

1 onion, sliced

3 tomatoes, roughly chopped

2 sprigs marjoram or oregano

1 teaspoon sweet pimentón

2 small garlic bulbs

500 g (1 lb 2 oz) baby potatoes

2 small marinated artichoke hearts, halved

freshly ground black pepper

Picada

3 small garlic cloves, grated

pinch of salt flakes

bunch of curly parsley, leaves picked and chopped

2 teaspoons dry white wine

80 ml (⅓ cup) olive oil

1½ tablespoons grapeseed oil

To make the picada, combine the ingredients in a bowl and set aside.

Blanch the lamb in a large saucepan of simmering salted water with one bay leaf for 40 minutes. In a separate saucepan of simmering salted water, add the chicken and another bay leaf and cook for 25 minutes. Strain the liquids into a large stockpot and set aside the lamb and chicken on a large plate. Simmer the broth for 30–40 minutes, until reduced by half.

Heat 1 tablespoon of the olive oil in a large heavy-based frying pan over high heat. Working in batches, sear the lamb and chicken on all sides, then transfer to a heavy-based stockpot. Cook the sausages in the same pan until golden on all sides, then transfer to the pot with the meat.

Dice the capsicums and add them to the frying pan, along with the onion, and cook over medium–low heat for 12–15 minutes, until soft and starting to colour. Add the tomato, another bay leaf, the marjoram or oregano and pimentón, and cook, stirring, for 6–8 minutes, until the tomato has broken down to a paste. Stir through half the picada and add 1.25 litres (5 cups) of the reserved broth. Bring to a simmer, then transfer to the pot with the meat.

Meanwhile, in a separate frying pan, heat the remaining oil over medium–low heat and add the garlic, potatoes and the remaining bay leaf. Sauté for 20–30 minutes, until the potatoes are cooked through and golden. Transfer the potatoes and garlic to a tray lined with paper towel to absorb any residual oil, then transfer to the pot with the meats and stock.

Still over medium–low heat, fry the artichoke for 2 minutes or until golden brown, then add to the pot. Stir through 2 tablespoons of the remaining picada and place the pot over medium–high heat. Bring to a simmer, season with salt and pepper, then cover and cook for 10 minutes to bring all the flavours together.

Serve on a large platter with the remaining picada spooned over the top.

There are many types of fideo pasta used in various *fideuà* dishes, particularly in Valencia, Catalonia and the Balearic provinces. *Fideo* is the Spanish word for noodle and while the Western world might be more familiar with pasta via the Italians, these short noodles feature in some of Spain's most famous dishes.

This stew tends to be served quite wet and the fideos are very well cooked. It's a comforting dish with the tasty sobrassada meatballs dotted among the soft pasta, and the mushrooms and cinnamon providing an earthy flavour. Cook it to your taste, but don't worry if you overcook the pasta, as that's how it's meant to be.

Fideuà con albondigas

150 g (5½ oz) day-old crustless sourdough bread, torn

2 tablespoons milk

200 g (7 oz) ground pork

200 g (7 oz) ground veal

100 g (3½ oz) sobrassada (see page 8)

1 large egg

1 teaspoon dried oregano

salt flakes and freshly cracked black pepper

60 ml (¼ cup) extra virgin olive oil

1.2 litres (41 fl oz) chicken stock

1 onion, chopped

3 garlic cloves, chopped

1 teaspoon sweet pimentón

1 teaspoon smoked pimentón

1 cinnamon stick

2 large tomatoes, grated

125 ml (½ cup) dry white wine

300 g (10½ oz) mixed mushrooms, roughly chopped

pinch of saffron threads

200 g (7 oz) thick fideos

200 g (7 oz) tinned butter (lima) beans, rinsed and drained

100 g (⅔ cup) frozen peas

4 sprigs of parsley, chopped

lemon wedges, to serve

crusty bread, to serve

Soak the bread in the milk in a small bowl for 5–10 minutes. Squeeze the milk from the bread and place the bread in a large bowl. Discard the milk.

Combine the pork, veal, sobrassada, egg and oregano in a bowl and season with salt and pepper. With wet hands, roll the mixture into golf ball–sized balls.

Heat 1 tablespoon of the olive oil in a large frying pan over medium–high heat and fry the meatballs, swirling the pan to help keep them round, for 6–8 minutes, until evenly browned. Remove from the pan and set aside on a plate.

Pour the chicken stock into a saucepan and bring to a gentle simmer over medium heat.

Meanwhile, add the remaining oil and the onion to the pan you cooked the meatballs in and cook for 8–10 minutes, until soft. Stir through the garlic, pimentóns and cinnamon stick and cook for a further 2 minutes, then add the grated tomato. Keep stirring, then pour in the wine and simmer until evaporated. Add the mushrooms and continue to cook until beginning to colour. Add the chicken stock and saffron and bring to a rapid simmer. Add the fideos and beans, then reduce the heat to a gentle simmer, cover and cook for 10–12 minutes. Return the meatballs to the pan, add the peas and continue to cook for 6–8 minutes, until heated through and the pasta is very well cooked.

Ladle into serving bowls and stir through the chopped parsley. Serve with lemon wedges on the side and tuck in with some crusty bread.

This dish is a combination of European cuisines, with the distinctly strong pork flavour pairing beautifully with the sweet cabbage and earthy mushrooms. The brining is not absolutely essential, but I love how it imparts even more flavour to the dish and prevents the loin from drying out, culminating in a moist, evenly cooked result every time.

Lomo de cerdo con col

1 kg (2 lb 3 oz) pork loin, skin on and scored

2 tablespoons light-flavoured extra virgin olive oil

salt flakes

¼ green or savoy cabbage, outer leaves removed

120 g (4½ oz) pancetta, diced

½ onion, finely diced

2 celery stalks, finely diced

¼ fennel bulb, finely diced, fronds reserved

3 garlic cloves, chopped

150 g (5½ oz) swiss brown or pine mushrooms, finely chopped

3 sprigs of thyme

150 ml (5 fl oz) dry sherry or dry white wine

750 ml (3 cups) chicken stock

crusty bread, to serve

Brine

1 tablespoon black or white peppercorns

1 tablespoon aniseed

1 tablespoon fennel seeds

70 g (2½ oz) sea salt

55 g (¼ cup) brown sugar

2 fresh bay leaves

250 ml (1 cup) boiling water

270 g (9½ oz) ice cubes

To make the brine, lightly toast the spices in a small frying pan over medium heat, until fragrant, then place in a large non-reactive dish with the salt, sugar and bay leaves. Pour in the boiling water. Stir until the salt and sugar have dissolved, then add the ice and stir until it has mostly melted. Add the pork, skin side up, and top with extra cold water to cover the loin (but not the skin), if necessary. Refrigerate the pork for 12 hours, then drain and thoroughly pat dry with paper towel. Set aside, uncovered, to continue drying.

Preheat the oven to 230°C (445°F) fan-forced.

Once the pork has come to room temperature, place it on a wire rack over a roasting tin, skin side up, and rub in half the olive oil and a good sprinkling of salt. Roast for 30–40 minutes, until starting to crackle on top. Reduce the heat to 170°C (340°F) and continue to cook for 40–45 minutes, until the juice of the loin runs clear when pierced with a skewer.

Meanwhile, cut the cabbage into four wedges with the core attached to hold the leaves together.

Heat the remaining oil in a large frying pan over high heat. Add the cabbage and cook for 4–6 minutes each side, until golden, then transfer to a large baking dish.

Reduce the heat to medium–high and fry off the pancetta for 4–5 minutes, until beginning to crisp, then add the onion, celery and fennel and cook for 12–15 minutes, until soft. Add the garlic, mushrooms and thyme and cook, stirring frequently, for 8–10 minutes, until golden. Pour in the sherry or wine and simmer until the liquid has reduced to a syrup. Add the stock, bring to the boil, then reduce the heat to medium and simmer for 15–20 minutes, until the liquid has reduced by half. Add to the dish with the cabbage.

Increase the oven temperature to 230°C (445°F). Roast the cabbage on the bottom shelf for 10 minutes or until soft.

Rest the pork for 12–15 minutes, then slice and divide among plates. Place the roasted cabbage on a serving platter, top with the fennel fronds and serve with crusty bread.

Outdo

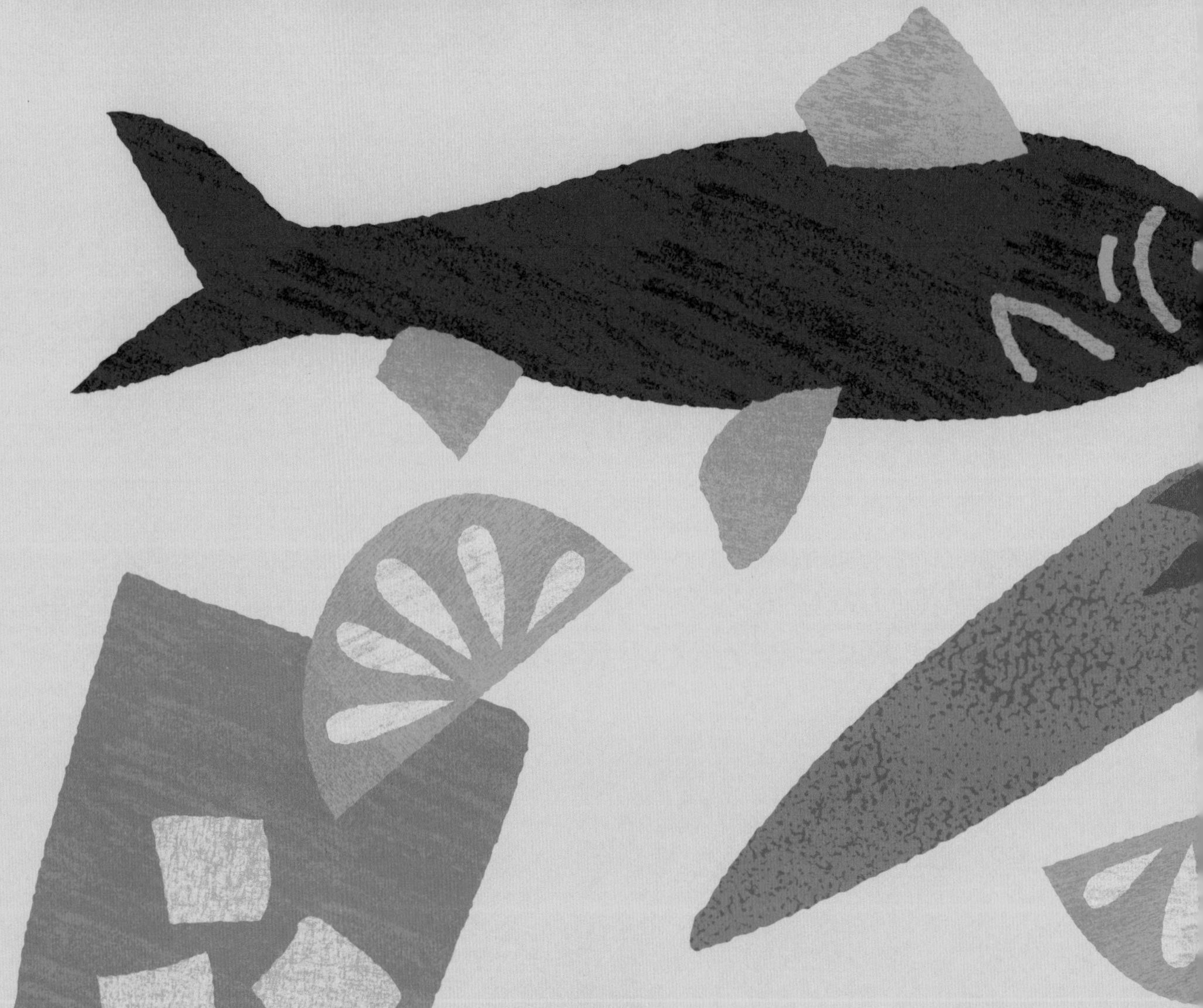

Gath

or

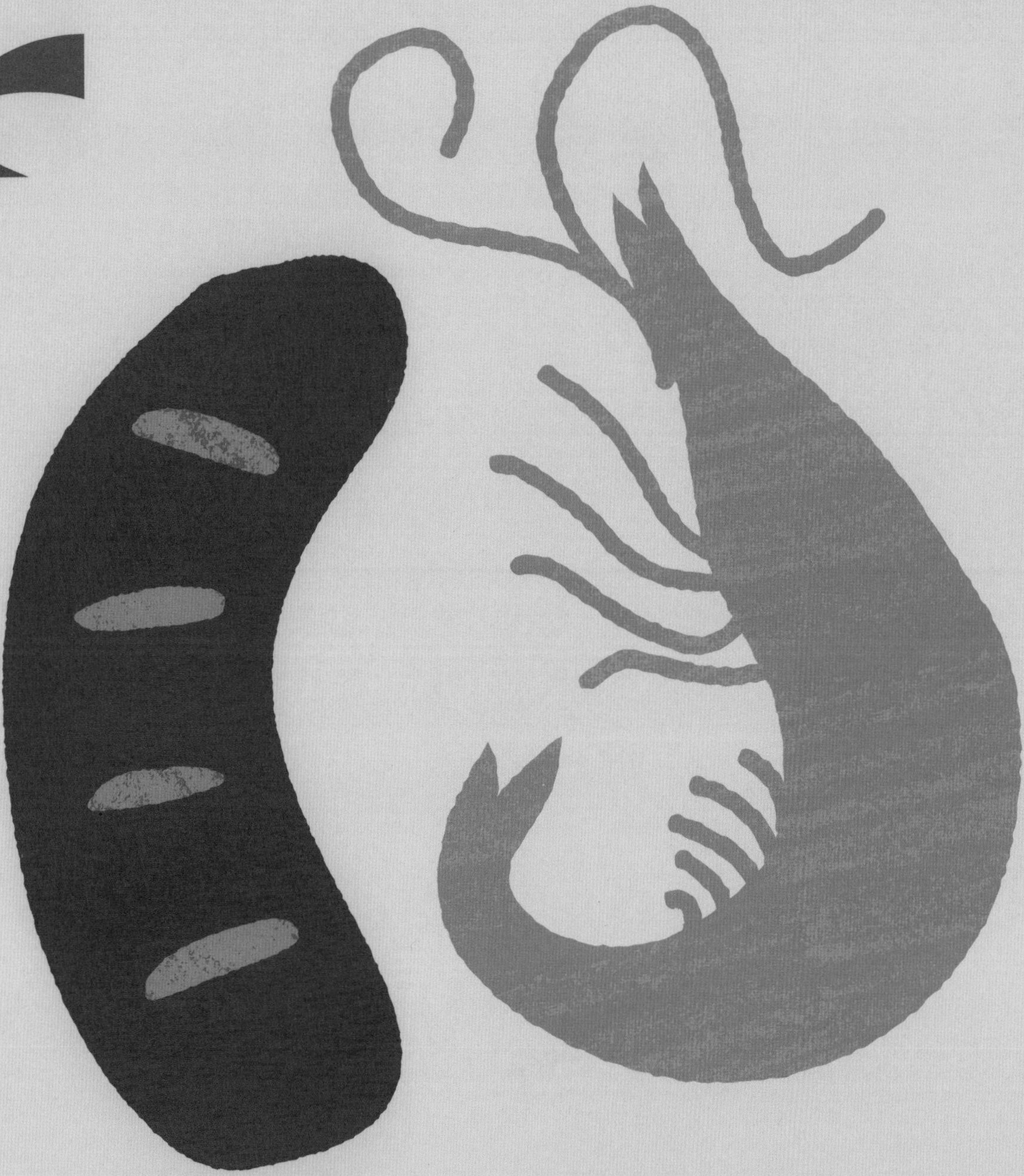

erings

 A cosy afternoon picnic is not something you will often see in Spain. Food neatly spread out on a cute tartan blanket, complete with wicker basket and wide-brimmed hat? No way! Instead, you are more likely to witness a *romeria*: a lively gathering that looks more like a scene from a Viking village party, with portable chairs, trestle tables, shade cloths of patchwork sheets and brightly coloured bunting strung up for a *fiesta* atmosphere.

Traditionally, these open-air celebrations would follow Sunday mass, with local worshippers walking in procession through the surrounding hills and into town where the feasting would begin. There, the aroma of chorizo and other local *embutidos* (charcuterie) sizzling on makeshift barbecues would fill the air, and kids and pets would run around playing until dusk, when, inevitably after a few drinks, dancing would begin.

Due to Spain's mild climate, outdoor gatherings are not limited to the summer months. In late winter in Catalonia, calçots (a type of salad onion that only grows in the region) bring people out in droves. Huddled around wood-fired barbecues, they cook these over-sized spring onions (scallions) until blackened and then wrap them in newspaper to steam.

Along the coast, seafood reigns supreme and prawns (shrimp), razor clams and sardines all feature regularly. Seared briefly over flames, they are eaten straight off the barbecue, with only a napkin for a plate, while usually balancing an ice-cold beer, cocktail or sangria in the other hand.

This chapter is all about catering for a big posse, where you can bring together friends and family, make some noise and eat the day away in true *romeria* style.

The *calçotada* is a truly unique, late wintertime culinary Catalan custom – a cult event on the calendar year. Calçots, a type of salad onion unique to the area, only grow between December and March, and their harvest results in festive gatherings at wood-fired barbecue settings under the first bursts of springtime sun.

A messy affair – bibs are worn like medals and wine is passed around in a traditional *porró* (a wine pitcher drunk straight from the spout) – the long, mini leek-like scallions are blackened on the barbecue and then wrapped tightly in porous newspaper to sweat, soften and sweeten. Traditionally served on a rooftop terracotta tile, the calçots' charred outer layers are peeled to reveal the white, soft flesh that is then dunked into the inseparable salvitxada and, with a tilted head, lowered into the mouth.

Calçots

6–8 bunches calçots (Catalan scallions), thick spring onions (scallions) or baby leeks

1 x quantity Salsa salvitxada (see page 261)

Fire up a charcoal or wood-fired barbecue 40–60 minutes before you want to start grilling. You want to get it to a point where the coals have stopped smoking and you can't hold your palm 15 cm (6 in) above the coals for more than 4 seconds without really feeling a sting.

Clean the calçots a little by cutting off the roots and washing any dirt away under running water. Trim some of the green tops if they're very long and stringy.

Place the calçots on the grill and allow each side to char and burn gradually, turning them every 4–6 minutes, for even cooking. The calçots will start to blister out some moisture and let off a sizzling hiss when they are ready.

Wrap the calçots in plenty of newspaper for 10 minutes to sweat, sweeten and impart all that charred flavour to the flesh.

Unwrap and serve on a large platter with the salvitxada in a few bowls scattered around the table. Calçots are often eaten while standing to get a better head tilt. Avoid any white tablecloths and invite people to wear bibs – they will thank you for it!

The pairing of crustaceans and cured ham is a cocktail party favourite around the world. The Spanish can be quite partial to a prawn (shrimp) head, and it's quite typical to see punters at restaurants or beach shacks slurping them like straws.

Serve these as a really quick and easy summer appetiser or offer them individually as canapés at your next party and see if anyone eats them like a true European!

Brochetas de gambas

2½ tablespoons extra virgin olive oil

zest and juice of ½ lemon

1 garlic clove, minced

2 teaspoons chopped parsley leaves

salt flakes and freshly cracked black pepper

8 green king prawns (jumbo shrimp), deveined, heads and tails left intact

8 thin slices of jamón

8 large metal or pre-soaked bamboo skewers

oil spray

In a bowl, combine the olive oil, lemon zest and juice, garlic, parsley and salt and pepper, to taste.

Rinse the prawns and pat dry with paper towel, then coat them in the marinade. Wrap the jamón around the middle of each prawn and slide them onto the skewers, through the tail and out the head.

Heat a barbecue grill plate to high. Spray the surface with oil and cook the prawns for 3–4 minutes each side, until the jamón is starting to crisp and the prawn flesh has turned pink.

Serve to go.

Mostly fished off the coast of Galicia, these long-shelled fingers of the sea are found on tapas menus all over the country. They can be hard to find outside the Iberian Peninsula, so if you don't mind an imported frozen product, then do give this dish a try. Otherwise, wait until your next trip to Spain, hit the local seafood market and cook up these sweet-tasting clams for your travelling crew, fresh and simple. Here, I've swapped out the typical parsley picada for island fennel flavours. Delicious!

Navajas a la plancha

1 teaspoon fennel seeds

3 garlic cloves, finely chopped

1 tablespoon extra virgin olive oil

80 ml (⅓ cup) dry white wine

pinch of salt flakes and freshly cracked black pepper

24 razor clams in their shells

2 fennel fronds or dill sprigs, fronds picked

Lightly toast the fennel seeds in a small frying pan over medium heat, until they just start to release their oils and begin to hiss in the pan. Transfer to a mortar and pestle and grind to a coarse powder. Place in a bowl with the garlic, half the olive oil, the wine and salt and pepper.

Heat a large heavy-based, well-seasoned flat griddle plate or gas barbecue flat plate on high until smoking hot. You will need to work in batches so have some paper towel handy to wipe the plate clean between each batch. Brush the plate with a little of the remaining oil and place the clams, hinge side down, on the plate. With tongs at the ready, turn them over as soon as they open and press down on the shells to flatten the flesh against the plate. Cook for 1 minute or until browned, then spoon over some of the dressing. Cover and steam the clams for a few seconds, then transfer to a plate and keep warm while you cook the rest, bringing the heat back up to high and applying another drizzle of oil before adding the next batch.

Drizzle the garlic and juices from the plate over the cooked clams and serve with the fennel or dill fronds scattered over the top.

Outdoor barbecue *fiestas* are a regular feature at household gatherings and in villages where *sardinas* are the main event. Locals might gather in the town square to celebrate a patron saint and the council will put on a big feast of sardines for everyone to enjoy, play a little flamenco and dance. The sardines are cooked covered in fig leaves to help steam them along and curb some of the fishy aroma! The leaves are then used as a biodegradable plate. This dish goes particularly well with the tomato salad on page 120.

Sardinas a la parilla

12–16 sardines, gutted and rinsed, patted dry with paper towel

10 fresh fig leaves (from a neighbour's tree if you're lucky), slightly dampened so they don't ignite

30 g (¼ cup) sultanas (golden raisins), roughly chopped

80 ml (⅓ cup) sherry vinegar or red wine vinegar

1 garlic clove, sliced

2 tablespoons capers, drained and rinsed

60 ml (¼ cup) extra virgin olive oil

zest of ¼ orange

1 teaspoon brandy

salt flakes and freshly cracked black pepper

2 tablespoons pine nuts, toasted

Fire up a charcoal or wood-fired barbecue 40–60 minutes before you want to start grilling. You want to get it to a point where the coals have stopped smoking and you can't hold your palm 15 cm (6 in) above the coals for more than 4 seconds without really feeling a sting.

Place the sardines on a grill over the coals, cover with the fig leaves and cook for 4–6 minutes, until the bottom of the fish is charred. Remove the leaves and turn the sardines over, then cover again and cook for a further 4–6 minutes.

Meanwhile, heat the sultanas, vinegar, garlic, capers and 2 tablespoons of water in a small saucepan over low heat for 4–6 minutes, until the sultanas have absorbed the water. Remove from the heat and set aside in a heatproof bowl to cool. Add the olive oil, orange zest and brandy, and season with salt and pepper. Mix through until you have a vinaigrette consistency.

Place the fig leaves on a large serving platter and top with the sardines. Drizzle with the sultana and caper sauce and sprinkle over the toasted pine nuts.

Ash-roasted vegetables

Traditionally, this dish is barbecued over coals. *Escalivar* means to cook in ashes or directly on hot embers, a technique also used for cooking Catalonia's famous *patates al caliu* (baked potatoes). In the past, Catalans didn't have access to an abundance of resources, such as gas, and even today a lot of homes still run off refillable *butano* (gas bottles). You can hear the peddlers banging bottles all day long and yelling 'butanoooooo' around the streets.

An oven can be used for this recipe, but it will sacrifice the taste and spirit of the dish. If you are cooking inside, a gas stovetop is a better option; just put some foil around the elements to avoid the mess. There are many ways to eat this dish: on its own with good-quality tinned sardines or anchovies, as a side for grilled fish or meats, or on top of the famous coca de verduras (see page 23).

Escalivada

2 large brown onions, unpeeled

2 eggplants (aubergines)

2 red capsicums (bell peppers)

1 garlic clove, thinly sliced

80 ml (⅓ cup) extra virgin olive oil

2 tablespoons Salsa verde (see page 259), for drizzling

salt flakes

Fire up a charcoal or wood-fired barbecue 40–60 minutes before you want to start grilling. You want to get it to a point where the coals have stopped smoking and you can't hold your palm 15 cm (6 in) above the coals for more than 4 seconds without really feeling a sting.

Using long tongs, first place the onions in the embers for 5–6 minutes, as they'll need a bit more time than the other ingredients. Make two or three pricks in the eggplants to prevent them exploding and carefully add to the embers, followed by the red capsicums. Using tongs, turn the vegetables often so they don't completely blacken or overcook on one side.

Meanwhile, combine the garlic and olive oil in a small jar and set aside to infuse.

When the vegetables have just softened and are well-coloured all over, carefully remove them from the embers, shake off as much ash as possible and place in a large stainless steel or heat-retaining bowl. Cover with plastic wrap or foil and let the vegetables carry on cooking internally for about 20 minutes. You don't want to overcook them on the embers or the flesh will fall apart and lose its sweetness.

Once cool enough to handle, gently peel the vegetables. Do not wash – use a blunt knife or the back of a spoon to remove any unwanted burnt bits. Cut the eggplant and capsicum into strips, separate the onion layers and arrange the vegetables on a serving platter.

Drizzle over the garlic oil and salsa verde, sprinkle with salt flakes and enjoy.

With so many wonderful beach-shack eateries around Spain, there's no better way to eat whole fish, straight from the makeshift outdoor chargrill and onto your plate after an afternoon swim. Sun, beach, sangria and grilled fish. Repeat. That's what summertime in Spain means.

So simple, yet not so easy to get right, the locals know their grilled fish. They send their fish 'back to the sea' by submerging them in a brine slurry before cooking. Apart from helping to season the fish from the outside in, this process also partially sets the proteins close to the surface of the skin, which prevents the fish from drying out and sticking when placed on the grill.

Pescado entero a la brasa

200 g (7 oz) fine sea salt

2 x 800 g (1 lb 12 oz) whole snapper, bream or sea bass, cleaned and gutted, scales left on

60 ml (¼ cup) sherry vinegar

25 g (1 oz) raisins

bunch of silverbeet (Swiss chard), stalks removed and leaves finely shredded

25 g (1 oz) pine nuts

1 small onion, finely diced

3 garlic cloves, thinly sliced

⅓ teaspoon ground cinnamon

pinch of freshly cracked black pepper

60 ml (¼ cup) extra virgin olive oil

lemon wedges, to serve

Make a slurry with the salt and 500 ml (2 cups) of water in a large non-reactive dish. Rub the fish all over with the salt water, as well as inside the cavity, then set aside at room temperature for 1 hour.

Prepare a charcoal grill for grilling in two zones. Keep one end burning quite intensely and the other end with a more moderate heat. Wait until the flames have died down and the coals have an even coating of white ash.

Meanwhile, bring the sherry vinegar and raisins to the boil in a small saucepan over medium heat, then remove from the heat and set aside.

Place the silverbeet in a large bowl with the pine nuts, onion, garlic, cinnamon, pepper and 2 teaspoons of the olive oil. Mix well to combine, then add the raisins and 2 teaspoons of the soaking vinegar.

Using paper towel, wipe the salt water from the fish until completely dry. Set aside for a further 15 minutes at room temperature to continue to air-dry.

Stuff the silverbeet mixture inside the cavities of both fish.

When the coals are ready, give the grill a good scrub with a grill brush, then season with a clean rag dabbed in a little of the oil (be careful it doesn't drip into the fire and flare up).

Rub the fish well with the remaining oil and gently place at the hot end of the grill. Cook for 6–10 minutes, until charred and the fish lifts easily from the grill. Gently flip the fish over and cook the other side for a further 6–10 minutes, until charred and cooked through. If the fish is still a little pink inside, but charred on the skin, transfer the fish to the cooler end of the grill to finish cooking.

Serve with lemon wedges and enjoy the crispy skin!

A good mixed grill is often served as the main course after a *calçotada* (see page 208), but don't let that stop you making this outside of calçot season. On the outskirts of Barcelona, you will find makeshift kitchen huts with huge outdoor grills, plastic outdoor furniture, chequered tablecloths, a *porrón* (pitcher) full of shandy set in the middle of the table and a few local dogs hanging around being shooed away with the same set of tongs used to flip the local *butifarra* (sausages). Groups of friends or families often make a day of it, travelling on the train from Barcelona to feast together for a long, messy lunch.

Carne asada a la parilla

2 potatoes, halved

2 artichokes or zucchini (courgettes), halved

1 x 300 g (10½ oz) veal cutlet

4 chicken or rabbit marylands (leg quarters)

4 lamb cutlets (caps left on)

4 pork and fennel sausages

2 black puddings

1 large cured chorizo

2 fresh chorizo sausages

2 red bullhorn peppers or red capsicums (bell peppers), halved, seeds removed

60 ml (¼ cup) extra virgin olive oil

salt flakes

Alioli (see page 256), to serve

Salsa salvitxada (see page 261), to serve

Fire up a charcoal or wood-fired barbecue 40–60 minutes before you want to start grilling. You want to get it to a point where the coals have stopped smoking and you can't hold your palm 15 cm (6 in) above the coals for more than 4 seconds without really feeling a sting.

Place all the vegetables and meats on a large tray and lightly cover with the olive oil.

Place a grill over the coals and put the potato halves and artichoke or zucchini in a moderately hot spot. They should start to colour up nicely after 10 minutes. You may need to move them around the grill until you find the perfect place.

Find the hottest part of the grill and cook the veal cutlet and chicken or rabbit for 10–12 minutes each side, then move to the side of the grill, away from the coals, to rest.

Place the lamb, sausages, black puddings and chorizos on the grill over an even heat and cook for 6–8 minutes. Remove anything that cooks more quickly and set aside on a baking tray in a warm spot near the barbecue to rest. You can always give it a blast at the end before serving.

Finally, add the peppers or capsicums and cook, turning three or four times for about 6 minutes each side, until the skins starts to colour and wrinkle.

Sprinkle the meats and vegetables with salt flakes and cut the veal cutlet and cured chorizo into four thick slices. Halve the fresh chorizos and black puddings and serve everything up on a large serving platter with plenty of alioli and salvitxada.

The capital of Menorca, Mahón, is home to the famous Xoriguer Gin. It is a surviving influence from the British occupation of Menorca in the 18th century, and apart from Plymouth it is the only gin with a Protected Designation of Origin. During the occupation, locals used what they had on hand to keep up with the sailors' demand for liquor, and many brewed with distilled wine rather than the usual grains. Xoriguer Gin is still made this way today in wood-fired copper stills, then rested in oak barrels before bottling, which gives it a distinctly bitter and smoky flavour of green wood, juniper and pepper.

These two gin cocktails are served ice-cold on beaches throughout the Balearics. *Pomada*, meaning 'ointment' in Catalan, is made with a cloudy, lemony lemonade and sometimes served as a slushy. For a drier experience, opt for the Pallofa, a beautifully simple gin and soda with a splash of lemon zest.

Pomada i Pallofa

Pomada

135 g (1 cup) small-cubed ice

200–250 ml (7–8½ fl oz) good-quality gin

150 ml (5 fl oz) freshly squeezed lemon juice

500–600 ml (17–20½ fl oz) good-quality lemon soda, to taste

2 thick lemon slices, quartered, plus extra slices to serve

Tip the ice into a jug and add the gin and lemon juice. Give everything a stir with a swizzle stick or chopstick, then pour in the lemon soda to taste.

Place two quartered lemon slices in four highball glasses and bruise with a wooden pestle or the end of a wooden spoon. Divide the drink evenly among the glasses and top with a few more slices of lemon. Serve with a little napkin and some salty bar snacks.

Pallofa

200 ml (7 fl oz) good-quality gin

600 ml (20½ fl oz) soda water (club soda)

4 strips of lemon peel

large ice cubes, to serve

Pour the gin into four rocks glasses. Top with the soda water, lemon peel and a few large ice cubes and serve straight away.

Thanks to the famous nightlife of Ibiza, the symbol of the double cherry has become a mascot for the island. Couple that with wine in the form of the famous Spanish party tipple sangria, and you have the perfect drink to take you back to that beach-club mood.

Sangria de cereza

180 g (6½ oz) fresh or frozen cherries, pitted and halved

750 ml (25½ fl oz) bottle red wine

200–250 ml (7–8½ fl oz) cherry brandy liqueur, such as kirsch

150 ml (5 fl oz) freshly squeezed orange juice

1 orange, thinly sliced

1 lime, thinly sliced

500–600 ml (17–20½ fl oz) lemon-lime soda

ice cubes, to serve

Combine the cherries, wine, cherry liqueur, orange juice and half the orange and lime slices in a jug. Stir to combine, then refrigerate for at least 2 hours or until completely chilled.

Pour in the soda, fill with ice and stir. Evenly divide among eight glasses, top with the remaining orange and lime slices and serve.

Sangria de cirera

Pomada

Pallofa

Sweet

Dulces

A lot of love and honour is dedicated to Spanish sweets, which are still viewed as the ultimate gesture of giving and hospitality. Many of Spain's most famous *dulces* were traditionally made in convents from simple pantry ingredients and perhaps an egg or two from the neighbourhood chickens. Different sweets were attributed to a patron saint, religious public holiday or celebration, making them rich in history and purpose.

Over time, these offerings incorporated ingredients introduced to Spain: sweet wine and honey from the Romans; almonds, sugarcane and oranges from the Moors; and later, chocolate from the Americas. These ingredients still feature heavily in Spain's modern sweets and desserts; their execution often simple, allowing the quality of the produce to shine.

Some of the sweets in this chapter are not restricted to the end of an evening meal, when you are just as likely to be offered a fruit platter or a wedge of manchego with quince paste. The lemon meringue tart and chocolate roulade are enjoyed at any time of day, perhaps with an afternoon espresso as a post-lunch pick-me-up.

During the week, homemade desserts may consist of poached pears with ice cream, a crema Catalana (Spain's answer to the French crème brûlée), or perhaps a ricotta cheesecake that can be put together in five minutes and gently baked in the oven while you eat dinner.

If you're catering for a crowd, then look no further than the buñuelos de viento. These light-as-air doughnuts were traditionally reserved for Lent, but don't let that stop you enjoying these sugary bite-sized balls doused in aniseed liqueur at every possible opportunity.

No matter the occasion, or however small or large the offering, these sweet *dulces* finish off an evening in true Spanish style.

This is surely one of the greatest food marriages – home-made quince paste and semi-firm manchego. Eat it as a snack or even for breakfast to get you going. You can use quince paste as a jam to fill pastries and cakes, loosen it down with boiling water to make a sauce, or spread it on toast with melted cheese on top, to get you through the winter months. It also goes without saying that quince paste is the perfect addition to any cheese board, plus it keeps for months.

Queso con membrillo

2 kg (4 lb 6 oz) quince, washed, peeled, cored and cut into wedges (reserve the peel from 2 quinces)

2 large strips of lemon peel

½ teaspoon vanilla bean paste

1 kg (2 lb 3 oz) caster (superfine) sugar

60 ml (¼ cup) lemon juice

oil spray

manchego or your favourite cheese, to serve

Place the quince in a large heavy-based saucepan and add enough cold water to cover the fruit by 2 cm (¾ in). Tie the quince peel in a square of muslin (cheese cloth) – this gives a richer colour and maximises the pectin – and add to the pan, along with the lemon peel and vanilla. Bring to the boil over medium–high heat, then reduce the heat to a simmer, cover and cook for 30–40 minutes, until the fruit is tender.

Strain the quince and discard the quince peel, then transfer to a blender and blitz the fruit and lemon peel to a smooth purée.

Return the purée to a clean non-stick saucepan and heat over medium–low heat. Add the sugar and stir through until dissolved, then add the lemon juice. Reduce the heat to as low as it can go and cook, stirring regularly, for 1½–2 hours, until the purée is thickened and starting to turn a rich burnt-orange, maroon colour.

Lightly spray a 23 cm (9 in) square tin with oil and line with baking paper or plastic wrap. Spoon the quince paste into the tin and smooth the surface using a rubber spatula.

Refrigerate for a minimum of 4 hours until set, before cutting into thick slices or triangles to serve with your favourite cheese.

Wrap the leftover quince paste in baking paper and plastic wrap and keep in the fridge for up to 2 months.

Mató, also known as *requesòn*, simply means curds, and this dish is an ode to the farm. If you are fortunate enough to have access to milk and honey direct from the source, this simple dessert will be even more special. I sometimes add a sprig of thyme or a fresh bay leaf to the milk while its heating, especially in winter, to give more depth of flavour. I also like to sprinkle over bee pollen at the end or you could add your favourite toasted nuts.

In some rural taverns, they serve this dish still warm on the plate – it's that fresh.

Miel y mato

1 litre (4 cups) full-cream
  (whole) goat's milk
juice of 1 lemon
100 g (3½ oz) honey
100 g (3½ oz) honeycomb
2 teaspoons bee pollen

Slowly bring the milk to a simmer in a heavy-based saucepan over medium heat. Remove from the heat. Pour the lemon juice into the hot milk and gently move the liquid around until it starts to separate. Set aside for 10 minutes to settle the curds.

Strain the curds into a fine sieve lined with muslin (cheesecloth), then set aside for 1–2 hours or place in the fridge for 4 hours if you prefer a firmer *mató*.

Divide among bowls, spoon over the honey and honeycomb and sprinkle with the pollen.

Catalan crème brûlée

The French compete with Catalonia for the origin of this famous dish; however, there are some small differences. Quicker, easier and cheaper than a crème brûlée, the Catalans cook out the egg a little further on the stovetop and set their custards in the fridge with the help of cornflour (corn starch), as historically many people didn't have access to ovens. They also use milk, not cream – another peasant compromise.

Crema Catalana

1 litre (4 cups) full-cream (whole) milk

1 cinnamon stick

peel of ½ lemon

peel of ½ orange

7 large egg yolks

200 g (7 oz) caster (superfine) sugar

3 tablespoons cornflour (corn starch)

Gently warm the milk, cinnamon and citrus peels in a saucepan over medium–low heat until just starting to simmer at the edge of the pan. Remove from the heat and allow to stand for 15 minutes for the flavours to infuse.

Whisk the egg yolks in a large heatproof bowl, then whisk in 150 g (5½ oz) of the sugar until creamy. Whisk in the cornflour until well combined.

Strain the warmed milk into a jug, then slowly pour into the egg mixture, whisking to combine.

Pour the custard back into a clean saucepan and return to medium–low heat, stirring constantly with a wooden spoon or silicon spatula. Allow to gently simmer and bubble, moving the custard constantly to avoid scrambling on the bottom.

When the custard is thick enough to coat the back of the spoon, remove the pan from the heat and strain the custard through a fine sieve. This will pick up any scrambled egg from the base of the saucepan.

Evenly divide the custard among 4–6 ramekins, leaving a 5 mm (¼ in) gap at the top of each ramekin. Transfer to a tray and allow to cool slightly before refrigerating for at least 4 hours or ideally overnight.

To serve, sprinkle the remaining sugar over the top of the custards and caramelise to a hard crust using a blow torch or sugar iron. You can also caramelise the set custards under the grill (broiler): place the custards in a baking dish half-filled with iced water, sprinkle the sugar over the ramekins and grill (broil) until well caramelised.

These aniseed doughnuts are known as *buñuelos de viento* (wind doughnuts) for their light, airy centres. Buñuelos are traditionally only eaten during Lent, but these days they're enjoyed year-round. You can't just stop at one! Give me a *buñuelos* and a coffee over a *churro* with chocolate any day!

Buñuelos de viento

300 ml (10 fl oz) full-cream (whole) milk, warmed

10 g (⅓ oz) fresh yeast (or 2 teaspoons active dried yeast)

100 g (3½ oz) caster (superfine) sugar

500 g (1 lb 2 oz) plain (all-purpose) flour, plus extra for dusting

1 apple, peeled and cored, finely grated

2 tablespoons aniseed

1 tablespoon coriander seeds, ground

¼ teaspoon fine salt

80 g (2¾ oz) butter, softened

3 whole eggs

zest of 1 lemon

1.5 litres (6 cups) neutral oil, for deep-frying

100 ml (3½ fl oz) anise liqueur, such as pernod, Anis del mono or ouzo

100 g (3½ fl oz) granulated sugar

Whisk the milk, yeast and a pinch of the caster sugar in a jug. Set aside for 10 minutes in a warm place.

Place the remaining caster sugar, flour, apple, aniseed, ground coriander seeds, salt, butter, eggs and lemon zest in the bowl of a stand mixer fitted with the paddle attachment. With the motor running on medium speed, gradually pour the milk and yeast mixture into the bowl and mix for 2–4 minutes, until you have a smooth, elastic dough.

Tip the dough into a large bowl, cover with plastic wrap and leave in a warm place for about 1½ hours, until doubled in size.

Heat the oil in a large heavy-based saucepan to 190°C (370°F) on a kitchen thermometer. Drop a pinch of dough into the oil – if it sizzles straight away the oil is ready (be careful not to let the oil become too hot, otherwise a crust will form around the doughnuts too quickly, leaving the centres raw and cold).

Fill a piping bag or large zip lock bag with the dough, snip off a corner and use scissors to cut short lengths of dough straight into the oil.

Working in batches, fry the doughnuts for 2–3 minutes each side, until golden. Transfer to a tray lined with paper towel to absorb the excess oil, then sprinkle with splashes of the liqueur. Transfer the doughnuts to a large bowl and toss through the granulated sugar while still warm.

Serve immediately with some sweet sherry, coffee or warm milk.

Queso Mahón' is a young, creamy, well-rounded cheddar-type cheese. It's named after the port of Mahón in Menorca, where the British, during their occupation of the island in the 18th century, brought across cattle for cheese production.

Mahón cheese has a salty, tangy and mineral taste due to the high sea salt content in the local grass pastures. It's ripened in caves for as little as two months for young cheese and up to 12 months for the salty, drier and harder Mahón reserva.

This dessert ticks all the boxes when you can't decide between a cheese board, fruit platter or sweet.

Manzanas rellenas

20 g (¾ oz) unsalted butter, softened

4 apples

120 g (4½ oz) aged Mahón reserva or 12 month-aged cheddar, grated

2 thyme sprigs, leaves finely chopped

salt flakes and freshly cracked black pepper

1 tablespoon Calvados or other brandy

10 hazelnuts, roasted, skinned and roughly chopped

Preheat the oven to 180°C (350°F) fan-forced. Grease a small baking tray with the butter and line with baking paper.

Slice the top quarter off each apple and set the tops aside. Carefully cut out the cores, keeping the bottoms of the apples intact.

Gently spoon out the apple flesh, leaving a 5 mm (¼ in) layer of apple behind. Place the apple flesh in a bowl with the cheese and thyme and season with salt and pepper. Mix well to combine and smash up any larger apple chunks using the back of a fork. Set aside in the fridge for 10 minutes.

Sprinkle 1 teaspoon of Calvados or other brandy into each hollowed-out apple and stuff to the top with the cheese mixture. Transfer the stuffed apples to the prepared tray, along with the apple tops, and sprinkle over the hazelnuts. Bake for 15–20 minutes, until the cheese is melted and bubbling.

Serve with a drizzle of the remaining juices in the baking tray.

Most of Spain's pears are grown in the Ebro Valley. South of the valley is the protected Priorat wine region, which produces excellent dry, minerally, earthy grapes used to make red varieties of Garnacha and Carignan, which match perfectly with the pears.

The ice cream takes me straight back to Catalonia, where the locally grown saffron (which has been exported from the region since the 15th century) is ranked the best in Europe. Its earthy, floral, musky taste paired with the richness of the anglaise ice cream and sharpness of the wine, make this dessert absolute bliss.

Peras con vino y helado de azarfan

4 corella or williams pears

peel and juice of 1 lemon

1 litre (4 cups) dry red wine

1 cinnamon stick

1 vanilla bean, split in half lengthways

150 g (5½ oz) caster (superfine) sugar

1 fresh bay leaf

Saffron ice cream

500 ml (2 cups) full-cream (whole) milk

2 pinches of saffron threads

2 tablespoons floral honey

5 egg yolks

80 g (2¾ oz) caster (superfine) sugar

1 teaspoon cornflour (corn starch)

½ teaspoon vanilla bean paste

200 g (7 oz) crème fraîche

To make the saffron ice cream, heat the milk and saffron in a saucepan over medium–high heat until just about to simmer. Stir through the honey and set aside.

Whisk the egg yolks in a heatproof bowl, then whisk through the sugar, cornflour and vanilla bean paste until thick and pale. Gradually whisk the warm milk into the egg mixture, then place over a saucepan of simmering water. Cook, stirring, for about 12 minutes, until the mixture thickens and coats the back of a wooden spoon, then strain through a fine sieve while still hot.

Allow to cool completely, then whisk through the crème fraîche. Set aside in the fridge for 4 hours or preferably overnight.

Line a 21 cm x 11 cm (8¼ in x 4¼ in) loaf (bar) tin with baking paper and place in the freezer to chill.

Churn the custard in an ice cream machine according to the manufacturer's instructions until thick and smooth. Scrape into the chilled loaf tin and freeze for 2 hours.

Peel the pears from the stalk down to the base, leaving the stalk intact. Place in a bowl and cover with cold water. Add the lemon juice.

Place the lemon peel, wine, cinnamon stick, vanilla bean and seeds, sugar and bay leaf in a saucepan over medium–high heat and stir to dissolve the sugar. Bring to the boil, then reduce the heat to a gentle simmer. Strain the pears and lower them into the simmering wine mixture.

Cut a circle of baking paper the same diameter as the pan and place it over the pears. If the pears continue to float, weigh them down with a small plate to completely submerge them under the liquid. Cook for 12–15 minutes, until softened.

Serve the pears with a little of their poaching liquid and two scoops of the saffron ice cream.

In Spanish, *flan* refers to what the French call crème caramel. Both countries compete for the origin of this dish; however, the French tend to make individual portions of this wobbly-set custard, while the Spanish go large! This sophisticated flan has a hint of almond extract, which pairs really well with the orange. It's simple to make, but it's worth starting the day before and letting the caramel set overnight in the fridge, to mellow out the eggy flavour.

Flan de naranja

zest of 4 oranges (reserve
1 zested orange to serve)

juice of ½ orange

220 g (8 oz) caster (superfine)
sugar

500 ml (2 cups) full-cream
(whole) milk

1 cinnamon stick, broken in half

3 large eggs

3 egg yolks

¼ teaspoon almond extract

boiling water

Preheat the oven to 160°C (320°F) fan-forced. Place a 23 cm (9 in) oval baking dish in a large deep roasting tin.

Combine the orange zest and juice in a small bowl and set aside for 5–10 minutes.

Heat half the caster sugar and 60 ml (¼ cup) of water in a small saucepan over medium–high heat and gently swirl the pan for 3–4 minutes, until the sugar turns a golden caramel colour. Pour the caramel into the base of the baking dish.

Gently warm the milk, cinnamon and orange zest liquid in a saucepan over medium–low heat until just starting to simmer. Remove from the heat and set aside to cool a little.

Whisk the eggs, egg yolks and almond extract in a large bowl, then add the remaining caster sugar and whisk until creamy and pale. Strain the orange milk into the egg mixture, whisking to combine. Pour the custard into the baking dish, then pour enough boiling water into the roasting tin to come half way up the side of the dish. Bake for 40–50 minutes, until the egg is just set and still a little wobbly in the centre. Gently shake the tin – if the flan is firm around the edge but still has a slight wobble in the middle, it's ready (it will continue to cook as it cools).

Carefully transfer the baking dish to a wire rack to cool for 30–40 minutes. Refrigerate overnight to chill and allow the egg to completely set and mellow in flavour.

To unmould, run a sharp knife around the edge of the caramel, then invert onto a lipped serving plate. (The trick is to expose the caramel to air. Once this happens, it will slide out quickly so be ready to catch it.)

Take the reserved zested orange and slice off the top and bottom. Place the orange flat on a chopping board and, using a sharp knife, slice off the peel and white pith. Slice into the orange either side of each segment and gently pull the segments to release them.

Scatter the orange segments over the caramel and serve with a glass of sweet Pedro Ximénez sherry.

The burnt Basque cheesecake may have a cult following around the world, but this humble version sticks to the original ingredient – ricotta – instead of the modern supermarket cream cheese. Mixing the cream and ricotta together essentially creates a homemade version of cream cheese, except without any gelatine or other thickening agents. The locals also don't burn their version – well not on purpose, anyway!

Historically an Easter dessert, this ricotta cheesecake is now enjoyed all year round as a go-to quick weeknight dessert if the kids deserve a treat.

Tarta de queso

20 g (¾ oz) unsalted butter, softened

500 g (1 lb 2 oz) full-cream (whole milk) firm ricotta

125 ml (½ cup) thick (double/heavy) cream

6 large eggs, beaten

250 g (9 oz) caster (superfine) sugar

zest of ¼ lemon, plus extra to serve

Preheat the oven to 180°C (350°F) fan-forced.

Grease a 25 cm (10 in) round earthenware or ovenproof dish with the butter.

Using a fork, mix the ricotta and cream in a large bowl until smooth. Slowly pour in the beaten egg and whisk until well combined and you can't see any lumps. Add the sugar and lemon zest and whisk until smooth.

Spoon the mixture into the prepared dish and bake for 35–40 minutes, until golden and a skewer inserted into the centre of the cheesecake comes out clean. Alternatively, if you want to serve it Basque-style, cook for 50–60 minutes, until the top is dark brown and almost burnt at the edge.

Sprinkle over a little extra lemon zest and serve with some fresh fruit on a hot day. Perfect!

Known by many different names around the world, but commonly referred to as the Swiss roll, this cake of thin sponge painted with jam or cream and rolled into a log is by no means indigenous to Switzerland. This chocolate interpretation is hugely popular in Spain, where it is sold in almost every cake shop and bakery throughout the country. Enjoy with coffee or for afternoon tea.

El brazo

butter, for greasing

200 g (7 oz) dark chocolate
(70% cocoa solids)

80 ml (⅓ cup) espresso

6 large eggs, separated

150 g (5½ oz) caster (superfine)
sugar

2 tablespoons cacao powder

1 tablespoon pure icing
(confectioners') sugar, plus
extra for dusting

1 tablespoon Pedro Ximénez
or other sweet sherry

185 ml (¾ cup) thickened
(whipping) cream

1 teaspoon vanilla bean paste

Preheat the oven to 160°C (320°F) fan-forced. Line a 29 cm x 24 cm x 3 cm (11½ in x 9½ in x 1¼ in) Swiss roll (jelly roll) tin with greased baking paper.

Place the chocolate and espresso in a heatproof bowl over simmering water. Stir until melted and smooth, then remove from the heat and set aside to cool slightly.

Using a stand mixer with the whisk attachment, or electric beaters, beat the egg yolks and sugar until fluffy and pale. Fold through the melted chocolate and coffee mixture until well combined.

In a separate bowl, beat the egg whites to soft peaks, then gently fold through the chocolate and egg mixture.

Pour onto the prepared tray and bake for 12–15 minutes, until cooked through. Turn the oven off, leave the tray inside and keep the oven door slightly ajar to let the moisture escape. Allow the cake to cool in the oven for 10–15 minutes.

Combine the cacao powder and icing sugar in a small bowl, then sprinkle onto a sheet of baking paper just larger than the cooked sponge. Turn the sponge out onto the prepared baking paper and peel off the top piece of paper. Allow to cool completely, then sprinkle over the sherry.

Whip the cream and vanilla bean paste in a bowl until firm, then evenly spread it over the sponge. Roll up the sponge, using the edges of the baking paper as a guide. Wrap the cake in plastic wrap and refrigerate for 1–2 hours before slicing and serving.

The British left this dish behind in Menorca and it's now a favourite in households and pastry shops. It's made with a cookie base and sweetened condensed milk – none of that French sweet pastry and cream bother, although they do turn to France for the meringue.

Tarta de limon

150 g (5½ oz) unsalted butter, softened, plus extra for greasing

375 g (12½ oz) plain milk biscuits (cookies), such as Marie or Nice

pinch of salt flakes

4 large free-range eggs, yolks and whites separated

zest of 1 lemon

120 ml (4 fl oz) freshly squeezed lemon juice

395 g (13½ oz) tin sweetened condensed milk

½ teaspoon cream of tartar

250 g (2 cups) pure icing (confectioners') sugar

Preheat the oven to 180°C (350°F) fan-forced. Grease a fluted 25 cm x 5.5 cm (10 in x 2¼ in) round flan (tart) tin with a removable base with a little butter.

Place the biscuits in a large bowl and crush using the end of a rolling pin or the base of a small bowl. Alternatively, for a finer result, blitz the biscuits in a food processor. Stir through the butter, salt and 2 tablespoons of warm water until evenly combined, then transfer the mixture to the base of the prepared tin. Using the base of a glass, evenly press the mixture into the base and side of the tin, then set aside in the fridge for 30 minutes to firm up.

Bake the tart shell for 10 minutes or until just beginning to brown around the edge. Remove from the oven and set aside to cool on a wire rack.

Using a hand-held whisk or a stand mixer, whisk the egg yolks, lemon zest and juice and the condensed milk until creamy and combined. Pour into the cooled tart shell and bake for 15 minutes or until lightly set. Set aside to cool on a wire rack, then refrigerate for 1–2 hours, until completely set.

Measure 250 g (9 oz) of the egg whites into a clean, dry bowl and whisk using a stand mixer or electric beaters on medium–low speed until soft peaks form. Increase the speed to high, add the cream of tartar and gradually add the sugar, 1 tablespoon at a time, in a slow, steady stream until incorporated and the meringue is thick, glossy and stays standing when you lift out the whisk.

Transfer the meringue to a piping bag and pipe it onto the top of the set lemon tart in any design you like.

Preheat a grill (broiler) to medium. Grill the tart on the middle shelf until starting to colour or use a blow torch to slightly burn the surface of the meringue.

Slice and serve!

Basics

The Spanish love this sauce as much as the Americans love their ketchup and the French their mustard. It is an essential at the table no matter what's on offer: seafood stews, grilled prawns (shrimp), squid-ink dishes, dry-roasted meats … the list goes on.

Here, I've included three versions of this famous condiment, so experiment and see which one you like best. The traditional method requires no egg and is simply an emulsification of garlic (al) and (i) oil (oli), but it demands patience and will-power; the suave uses cooked garlic making it a little easier to digest, while the moderna is perfect for those who are simply short on time and equipment.

Alioli

Traditional

5 garlic cloves, germ removed, thinly sliced

½ teaspoon salt flakes

½ teaspoon lemon juice

60 ml (¼ cup) light-tasting olive oil

Suave

1 garlic bulb

pinch of salt flakes

1 egg yolk, at room temperature

125 ml (½ cup) extra virgin olive oil

½ teaspoon lemon juice

Moderna

125 g (½ cup) whole egg mayonnaise

3 garlic cloves, minced or finely grated

⅓ teaspoon salt flakes

½ teaspoon sherry vinegar

To make the traditional alioli, pound the garlic and salt using a mortar and pestle to a fine, wet paste. Squeeze in the lemon juice and mix to combine. Gradually add the olive oil, ½ teaspoon at a time, mixing and pulverising vigorously until completely emulsified. Add a splash of water at the end if you would like a slightly runnier alioli.

To make the suave, preheat the oven to 190°C (375°F) fan-forced.

Cut the top 5 mm (¼ in) off the garlic bulb, to expose the cloves. Sprinkle with salt and wrap tightly in foil. Bake for 25–30 minutes, until the garlic is caramelised and the cloves are popping up out of their skins. Allow to cool, then turn upside down and squeeze the flesh into a mortar and pestle or small bowl. Add the salt and egg yolk and mix through to combine. Gradually whisk in the olive oil, 1 teaspoon at a time, until you have a smooth alioli. Season with the lemon juice.

To make the moderna, place all the ingredients in a bowl and mix until thoroughly combined.

Keep the alioli in an airtight container in the fridge for 3–4 days.

Around the time of the 1992 Olympics the use of raw egg yolk was banned in hospitality outlets. Instead of teaching people how to properly handle and store fresh mayonnaise, pasteurised, liquidised egg yolks were made and sold in Tetra Brik cartons, which are still used today. I guess we can be thankful that Spain has other more relaxed regulations, such as those that allow you to visit a bar filled with plates of beautifully displayed pintxos, uncovered for you to help yourself.

Although not allowed in the hospitality world, you can still find some old-school restaurants and new-school modern chefs serving up mayo' the old way.

Mayonesa

1 egg yolk

1 whole egg

1 tablespoon sherry vinegar

pinch of salt flakes

80 ml (⅓ cup) grapeseed oil

60 ml (¼ cup) extra virgin olive oil

In a large bowl, whisk the egg yolk and egg, then incorporate the sherry vinegar and salt. Whisking constantly, gradually pour in the oils in a thin steady stream, until you have a thick mayonnaise. Alternatively, you can make the mayonnaise in the small bowl of a food processor or with a hand-held blender.

Keep the mayonesa in an airtight container in the fridge for 3–4 days.

This tomato sauce is the base, the backbone, the primrose path to braises, sautés and various paellas. Make a large batch, portion it up and keep it on hand in the freezer to add depth of flavour to your favourite dishes.

Roma (plum) tomatoes are the first choice here, but any ripe, mature red tomato will do. These are also best grated, but if you're pressed for time or want to make this in the middle of winter and can't access ripe tomatoes, then you can use the same weight in tinned chopped or diced tomatoes.

Sofrito

300 ml (10 fl oz) extra virgin olive oil

4 onions, finely diced

1½ teaspoons salt flakes

6 garlic cloves, finely grated

800 g (1 lb 12 oz) roma (plum) tomatoes, coarsely grated, skins discarded

250 ml (1 cup) dry sherry

Heat the olive oil in a large heavy-based saucepan or paella pan over medium heat. Add the onion and stir it through the oil. Bring the mixture to a gentle simmer, then reduce the heat to medium–low and cook, stirring often, for about 10 minutes, until the onion is translucent. Add the salt and continue to gently cook the onion, stirring, for a further 15 minutes or until golden. Add the garlic and cook for another 15 minutes or so, until all the moisture has evaporated and only the caramelised onion, garlic and oil are left in the pan.

Add the grated tomato and increase the heat to medium until the mixture starts to simmer. Continue to cook for 30 minutes, stirring the sofrito, as it reduces and the liquid evaporates. Reduce the heat to low and cover, stirring occasionally, for 20–30 minutes, until the sauce starts to turn a dark golden, chocolatey colour. Remove the lid, add the sherry and increase the heat to medium–high for the last 5 minutes of cooking, until all the alcohol has evaporated.

Set aside to cool completely. Store in an airtight container in the fridge for up to 2 weeks or divide into portions and store in the freezer for up to 2 months.

This quick little dressing has been around since medieval times and can be put on top of almost anything, from pan-fried fish and large cuts of roasted meats to grilled vegetables, or even used as a base for vinaigrettes.

For me, curly-leaf parsley works better here as it has a much earthier flavour and less moisture than its flat-leaf cousin. You can use any other herbs you like with the parsley – chervil is fantastic if you can get it.

Some recipes include bread and almonds as well, but I like to leave them out to keep the salsa lighter and more versatile as an accompaniment. My mother-in-law used to keep a bottle of left-over Cava in the fridge door and add any unfinished last drops of a variety of white wines to use in this salsa. She'd add to it, use it, add to it, use it – the same bottle for years! It was the best version I've ever had.

Salsa verde

3 small garlic cloves

pinch of salt flakes

bunch of curly-leaf parsley, leaves chopped

2 sprigs of chervil, marjoram or oregano, leaves chopped

3–4 mint leaves, finely chopped

2 teaspoons dry white wine (or 1 teaspoon white wine vinegar)

80 ml (⅓ cup) light-tasting extra virgin olive oil

60 ml (¼ cup) grapeseed or sunflower oil

salt flakes and freshly cracked black pepper

Using a mortar and pestle, pound the garlic with the salt to a paste. Add the herbs, one by one, and lightly bruise them into the garlic between each addition. Pour in the wine or vinegar and gently pound into the herbs, then gradually add the oils, stirring around the mortar to incorporate. Season to taste and serve straight away, or even better let it sit for a few hours before using.

You can also make this salsa in a food processor on pulse, but you don't want it to be a homogenised pesto-like sauce. It's nice when the herbs pool in the liquid a little when you drizzle it over your favourite dish.

The salsa verde will keep in the fridge for 1–2 days.

Picada is essentially a fresh paste used at the end of the cooking process to add texture, depth of flavour and an extra dimension to otherwise simple peasant dishes.

There are a few picadas in the Spanish repertoire and many, such as this one, can be adapted to match what you're serving it with. Toasted saffron threads can be added to accompany fish dishes or chocolate to deepen meat braises, while the nut combinations can be changed for pine nuts, pistachios or even toasted pumpkin seeds (pepitas) for a more modern twist, along with different types of herbs and spices.

This recipe is my standard go-to, which I play around with from time to time, depending on the ultimate result I'm looking for.

Picada

2 tablespoons extra virgin olive oil, plus extra for drizzling

3 garlic cloves, finely chopped

2 thin slices of white bread or baguette, cut into small cubes

40 g (¼ cup) blanched almonds, toasted

35 g (¼ cup) hazelnuts, roasted, skins rubbed off

½ teaspoon mild chilli powder (optional)

Heat the olive oil in a frying pan over medium heat and sauté the garlic and bread for 6–8 minutes, until golden.

Place the nuts, chilli powder, if using, garlic and bread in a food processor. With the motor running, drizzle in a little olive oil and blend until you have a thick, sticky paste.

Stir the picada through any number of the dishes in this book, or use it to thicken your favourite winter stew.

The picada will keep in an airtight container in the fridge for up to 10 days.

Some people claim that romesco and salvitxada are the same sauce, just identified differently depending on what they are accompanied with: salvitxada is only ever served with calçots (see page 208), while romesco is an integral part of the coastal winter salad xatonada (see page 125). Others argue that salvitxada does not contain bread and that this is the difference. I've included both recipes here for argument's sake, but every village and household has their way – some like it with a lot of vinegar while others like it strong in garlic. The variations are endless, so mix and match to suit your own taste.

Salsa salvitxada y salsa romesco

Salsa salvitxada

2–3 dried ñora peppers
(see page 8)

4 ripe tomatoes

100 g (3½ oz) blanched
almonds, toasted

50 g (1¾ oz) roasted hazelnuts

1 garlic clove, peeled

1 tablespoon sherry vinegar

salt flakes and freshly cracked
black pepper

100 ml (3½ fl oz) extra virgin
olive oil

Salsa romesco

1 garlic bulb, cut in half
crossways, plus 1 garlic
clove, peeled

salt flakes and black pepper

2 tomatoes

1 red capsicum (bell pepper)

½ white onion, unpeeled

1 piece of thickly sliced bread

2 tablespoons sherry vinegar

40 g (¼ cup) blanched almonds,
toasted

35 g (1¼ oz) roasted hazelnuts

2 teaspoons sweet pimentón

80 ml (⅓ cup) extra virgin
olive oil

To make the salsa salvitxada, rehydrate the ñora peppers in hot water until soft, then drain, slice open and remove and discard the seeds. Scrape the flesh from the skins into a bowl.

Heat a barbecue grill plate to high. Blister the tomatoes until the skins peel away, then peel and discard the skins.

Blitz the nuts in a food processor, then add the garlic, vinegar, pepper flesh, 1 teaspoon of salt, ½ teaspoon of pepper and the peeled tomatoes. Blitz again then, with the motor running, slowly add the oil until well combined. Incorporate a little water if you prefer a thinner consistency. The sauce will keep in an airtight container in the fridge for 4–5 days.

To make the salsa romesco, preheat the oven to 200°C (400°F) fan-forced. Place the garlic on a sheet of foil and sprinkle with salt. Wrap the garlic bulb halves in the foil, then transfer to the oven and bake for 30–40 minutes, until caramelised and the cloves are popping up out of their skins. Set aside to cool, then squeeze the garlic flesh into a bowl.

Heat a barbecue grill plate to high and char the tomatoes, capsicum and onion until the skins start to burn slightly and moisture begins to seep out. Remove from the heat, place the capsicum in a small bowl and cover with plastic wrap. Peel the tomatoes and onion.

Toast the bread in a frying pan or on the grill plate, then rub the remaining garlic clove over the toast. Transfer to a bowl and soak the bread in the sherry vinegar and 1 tablespoon of water.

Peel and deseed the capsicum, then place it in a blender with the tomato, onion, soaked toast, roasted garlic, nuts, pimentón and 1 teaspoon of salt. Blitz until well combined then, with the motor running, slowly pour in the oil. Incorporate a little water if you would like a thinner consistency and season to taste with black pepper. The sauce will keep in an airtight container in the fridge for 4–5 days.

It's typical to see *pescado de roca* (small rock fish) varieties piled up in huge mounds at the market for making stock. This combination of whole non-oily, small-boned fish, with internals that haven't quite developed yet, make for a clean, sweet result.

The heads and bones of larger white-fleshed non-oily fish, such as monkfish, cod or red mullet and snapper, are then mixed into the pot with the baby fish to add a saltier, fishier depth of flavour.

It's important not to overcook your fish stock. You want to extract the gelatine and flavour without leaching too much from the actual bones, which are more delicate than animal bones and can transfer a bitter taste to your stock when cooked for a long time. It's, therefore, important to cut your vegetables into smaller pieces to allow for the shorter cooking time.

Caldo de pescado

2 kg (4 lb 6 oz) large fish heads, bones, fins and tails (monkfish, cod, red mullet or snapper)

500 g (1 lb 2 oz) medium whole whitebait

2 tablespoons fine sea salt

1 leek, white part only, split in half lengthways, rinsed and sliced

2 brown onions, each chopped into 8 chunks

2 celery stalks, chopped into 3 cm (1¼ in) chunks

1 fresh bay leaf

8 white peppercorns

60 ml (¼ cup) dry white wine

3 sprigs of parsley

Soak the fish heads, bones, fins, tails and whitebait with the salt in a large bowl of cold water for 30 minutes. Drain and rinse well under cold running water, making sure you remove any blood from the larger spinal bones.

Transfer the fish to a large saucepan or stockpot with the remaining ingredients except the parsley and cover with 6 litres (6½ qts) of cold water. Bring to a simmer over medium heat and skim off any impurities that rise to the surface. Simmer for 20 minutes, then remove from the heat, add the parsley and allow to steep for 15 minutes. Strain the stock through a fine-mesh sieve and allow to cool completely.

Store the cold stock in the fridge for 3–4 days or in the freezer in batches for up to 3 months.

This stock owes its name to its dark colour, which is achieved by roasting bones and vegetables to caramelise the proteins and extract a richer, deeper flavour. It is an essential ingredient in a vegetable-thickened *demi-glace* or mother sauce that's used throughout the culinary world in traditional French-schooled kitchens. It's also perfect for stews, casseroles and meat-based rice dishes.

The smaller the pieces of bone, the faster you'll extract the flavour and gelatine.

Fondo oscuro de ternera

4 kg (8 lb 13 oz) veal or lamb bones (or a mixture), sawn into 5 cm (2 in) pieces (ask your butcher to do this for you)

2 garlic bulbs, cut in half crossways

2 brown onions, halved

3 celery stalks, halved

2 carrots, quartered

2 tablespoons tomato paste (concentrated purée)

4 dried porcini mushrooms

2 fresh bay leaves

3 sprigs of thyme

1 tablespoon black peppercorns

½ bunch of parsley stalks

250 ml (1 cup) dry white wine

Thoroughly rinse the bones under cold running water. Set aside to air-dry on a clean tea towel.

Preheat the oven to 200°C (400°F) fan-forced.

Transfer the bones to a large roasting tin and roast for 30 minutes. Rotate the tin, then chuck in the garlic and give the bones a stir so they brown evenly. Cook for a further 30 minutes, or until the bones start to crisp and turn a dark golden colour. Add the vegetables and tomato paste, give everything another stir and roast for a further 40 minutes.

Transfer the roasted bones, garlic and vegetables to a large stockpot and cover with 8 litres (8½ qts) of water. (Alternatively use half chicken stock and half water for a more decadent, richer result.) Add the dried porcini mushrooms, bay leaves, thyme, peppercorns and parsley stalks.

Place the roasting tin on the stovetop over medium–high heat and deglaze the tin with the white wine and 250 ml (1 cup) of water, scraping up the caramelised residual crispy bits from the bottom of the tin. Pour this mixture into the stockpot and slowly bring to a gentle boil, then reduce the heat to low and simmer for 4–6 hours, regularly skimming off any impurities that rise to the surface.

Remove from the heat and allow to steep for 1 hour before straining through a fine-mesh sieve. Allow to completely cool, then store in the fridge for 3–4 days or in the freezer in batches for up to 3 months.

Note
For an even richer stock to use for sauces, gravys or glazes, reduce the stock by another half over a very low simmer.

About the author

Emma Warren studied horticultural science at university before transferring her love of the veggie patch to the kitchen. She moved to Spain in 2001 and immersed herself in the world of Spanish culture, language and cuisine. Travelling the regions extensively from north to south, building edible gardens while Woofing (Working on Organic Farms), Emma began to spend more of her time in Spanish home kitchens before finally settling in Barcelona.

Emma's first experience in a commercial kitchen was at the popular cafe Kasparo, in the heart of El Raval, which focused on market-driven, seasonal and local produce. Emma ran the kitchen as head chef for three years, dedicating her summer-break months to honing her culinary skills at a boutique hotel in Mallorca, under several established British chefs. She returned home to Melbourne, Australia, to set up the kitchen Hogar Español at the iconic Spanish Club on Johnston Street in Fitzroy – a cult institution and live-music venue, where Spanish expats and the local community came together.

Emma soon returned to Spain to live permanently in the coastal town of Castelldefels, where she worked at a local four-star hotel which became a major training ground for mastering traditional French and Catalan cooking.

Years later, back in Melbourne, Emma completed her Australian commercial chef qualification and began working for some of Australia's top chefs, including Philippa Sibley and Karen Martini, as well as food personality Matt Preston, and recipe writing and product development for some of Australia's best-loved brands.

Today she resides on the Mornington Peninsula and juggles her days between her small son and freelance chef project work, while completing a bachelor of education in food technology and design.

Index

Published in 2022 by Smith Street Books
Naarm | Melbourne | Australia
smithstreetbooks.com

ISBN: 978-1-922417-90-9

Publisher: Lucy Heaver, Tusk Studio
Designer and illustrator: George Saad
Typesetter: Heather Menzies, Studio31 Graphics
Photographer: Rochelle Eagle
Food stylist: Lee Blaylock
Home economists: Emma Warren, Rachael Lane, Gabrielle Evans,
  Meryl Batlle, Josh Nicholson
Proofreader: Hannah Koelmeyer
Indexer: Helena Holmgren

Recipes in this book have previously appeared in *The Catalan Kitchen* and *Islas*.

Printed & bound in China by C&C Offset Printing Co., Ltd.

Book 233
10 9 8 7 6 5 4 3 2 1